Raincity:
Vancouver Reflections

**By the same author**

*New Moon and Money* (poems)
*The Blue Parrot*
*Three of a Kind* (three short novels)
*The Flea Market*

# Raincity:
## Vancouver Reflections

By John Moore

ANVIL PRESS ~ VANCOUVER

Copyright © 2020 by John Moore

All rights reserved. No part of this book may be reproduced by any means without the prior written permission of the publisher, with the exception of brief passages in reviews. Any request for photocopying or other reprographic copying of any part of this book must be directed in writing to Access Copyright: The Canadian Copyright Licensing Agency, One Yonge Street, Suite 800, Toronto, Ontario, Canada, M5E 1E5.

Anvil Press Publishers Inc.
P.O. Box 3008, Main Post Office
Vancouver, B.C. V6B 3X5 CANADA
www.anvilpress.com

Library and Archives Canada Cataloguing in Publication

Title: Rain city : Vancouver reflections / by John Moore.
Names: Moore, John, 1950- author.
Identifiers: Canadiana 20190103515 | ISBN 9781772141399 (softcover)
Subjects: LCSH: Moore, John, 1950- —Anecdotes. | CSH: Authors, Canadian (English)—Anecdotes | LCSH: Journalists—British Columbia—Vancouver—Anecdotes. | LCSH: Vancouver (B.C.)—Anecdotes.
Classification: LCC PS8576.O6142 Z46 2019 | DDC C818/.5403—dc23

Cover design by Rayola.com
Interior by HeimatHouse
Author photo by Joe Moore
Represented in Canada by Publishers Group Canada
Distributed by Raincoast Books

The publisher gratefully acknowledges the financial assistance of the Canada Council for the Arts, the Canada Book Fund, and the Province of British Columbia through the B.C. Arts Council and the Book Publishing Tax Credit.

PRINTED AND BOUND IN CANADA

*For Jean Clifford
who taught me how to write an essay
so I'd know what rules to break—
and the editors who let me get away with it.*

## Author's note:

All of these fugitive pieces appeared in print media at various times during the last thirty years. They have all been re-written, expanded, chopped, channelled, hot-rodded, Botoxed and surgically enhanced to an extent not possible when they originally appeared, despite the degree of editorial indulgence they enjoyed.

I've kept them around and worked on them from time to time because they each have the core of an idea, something about the city where I've lived most of my life, that has made them a way of touching base with myself that seemed less trivial than keeping a diary. Since I may be among the last generation of freelance journalists to enter the job like a rat coming up the toilet drain, instead of via college courses in media writing, they may have a small claim on history.

The precarious life of a free lance, would not have been possible without the patience and support of other writers, editors, publishers, friends, my extended family, Mary, Will, Joe, Tricia, and the dogs, cats, budgies and the whole mob.

—JM

Raincity: another name for Vancouver, BC.
—The Urban Dictionary

"Each of us carries mental place maps within us—maps that often bear little resemblance to reality...These imagined maps are distortions, yet for the individual they are truer depictions than those of cartographers."
—Witold Rybczynski

"A journalist is a reporter who can't hold a steady job."
—Paul St. Pierre

## Contents:

1. Village People / 11
2. A Walk on the Wild Side / 35
3. Imaginary Geography / 51
4. Bad Haircuts / 77
5. The Skin Trade / 95
6. Raincity Style / 111
7. Prozac.calm / 125
8. Finding My Marbles / 133
9. Sukiyaki / 145
10. Last Call for Alcohol / 155
11. Roadkill / 175
12. Crash Test Dummy / 183
13. Collecting for the Apocalypse / 195
14. A 29 Hand / 205
15. Last Resort / 219
16. *! (boom) / 235

Acknowledgments / 253
About the Author / 254

# ONE

# Village People

"What can you do? (shrug) It's progress."

"Yeah, (shrug) I guess."

This exchange between citizens contemplating recent grand openings of gigantic, generic side-by-side Wal-Mart and Home Depot units in Squamish, B.C. wasn't overheard in the kind of chrome-and-formica diner where liver and onions with mashed potatoes and gravy would not only be the dinner special, it would be sold out if you were one of those swells who dine after six. It was eavesdropped in the Squamish Tim Hortons, a national donut and coffee chain unit every bit as generic as the major retailers it now calls neighbours, itself in the process of grinding the old Mom & Pop local joints into cultural as well as financial oblivion.

'Progress' is the party dress small towns put on when they're about to drink too much cheap fizz and lie down for some slick developer from the Big Smoke. A decade ago, Squamish still crossed its legs when national corporate retailers like Loblaws and London Drugs tried to shove their sweaty hands up its civic skirt. In 2000, Loblaws' feelers toward putting a Superstore on one of the coveted intersection corners of the Sea to Sky Highway to Whistler were rebuffed with outrage at the suggestion the town wanted to become a 'big box' community.

Within a year of Loblaws' pitch, the site was home to a Canadian Tire outlet. Within five, Timbits was the town's brunch of choice, Wal-Mart and Home Depot were blueprinted and the highwayside Industrial Park, once home to heavy-duty mechanics and steel fabricators serving the logging and milling industry, was evolving into a commercial strip mall. The old downtown retail core that was a vibrant village community when we moved here in 1994 bemoaned a 30% vacancy rate and looked like the set of one of those post-nuclear dystopia movies of the 1960s.

We are "a town in transition" our newspaper constantly reminds us, spewing the mix of pathetic boosterism and platitudinous concern that substitutes for a genuine politics of engagement nationwide. Overwhelmed, all the municipal building inspectors threw in the towel in December 2006. Developers built on without permits. Two hypocrites even had the gall to claim in *The Squamish Chief* that any reform of the oversight process would affect their bottom line and "be detrimental to the town since it would reduce the availability of *affordable housing*," (italics mine). Meanwhile, they forged ahead, slapping up monster houses and luxury condos with nary a discouraging word from the pro-development municipal council. Council, after all, represents the electorate—we who now sit in Tim Hortons bitching about construction and grousing because the town isn't like it used to be—every one of our gripes tempered with guilty delight at having received tax assessments that inflate the value our properties almost to par with those of Vancouver's North Shore.

## Urban Hell

Squamish isn't some isolated minnow being gobbled by Shark City. The growth of cities is a historical inevitability. Rome, Paris, and London grew over centuries, millennia, absorbing surrounding communities that once were independent towns and villages. Flip through the maps of Bruce Macdonald's *Vancouver: A Visual History* (Talonbooks, 1992) and you'll see an illuminating time-lapse replay of the pattern as Vancouver morphed from a couple of sawmill-and-saloon outposts into Greater Vancouver, swallowing Burnaby, Richmond, Surrey, Delta, Ladner, Newton, Whalley, Port Moody. Even New Westminster, the Royal City that once aspired to be the Provincial capital, is now just Vancouver burb. Around the towns of the Fraser Valley, all the way to Mission, the chain of connecting roads, malls and in-fill housing developments grows tighter every year, not just linking them, but *binding* them to Vancouver.

Problems accompanying urban growth are fodder for daily headlines worldwide—jammed traffic, waste excreted by a mega-polis that paves over its own agricultural hinterland and becomes totally dependent on fuel, energy, and food imported from Elsewhere, land values ballooned by speculation, property taxes inflated by the expense of maintaining over-stressed and over-extended infrastructure and policing crime among a swelling underclass who can't afford to live decently in their own city.

In February 2007 the *Squamish Chief* reported, "Families throughout the community are facing growing affordable housing challenges and the thousands of new units proposed for Squamish won't help, according to a district-commissioned report." Even though almost 6000 new housing units were set to hit the market, the study conducted by City Spaces concluded that "For couple family households earning eighty percent of the median income, *none* of the new single detached housing or new townhouse product will be affordable. Many apartment units will have higher prices and will not be affordable as unit sizes will be larger, projects will be located on the waterfront, or projects will be constructed using concrete or steel (not wood)." Apparently lack of oversight didn't reduce those Squamish developers' bottom line enough. Welcome to *Greater* Vancouver: Squamish.

Essayist Walter Benjamin declared Paris the "capital of the 19th century"; a city that embodied the *zeitgeist* of a historical period, even though London was its true political and financial nexus. Few would argue that the only serious contender for the title of "capital of the 20th century" was New York. Never mind that this archetypal modern city was a nickel away from bankruptcy for most of the last half of its ten decades of fame as a result of dealing with the problems listed above. In the first decades of the 21st century, New York still remains the Big Apple, model for city fathers, planners, and media whores obsessed with being in at the birth of their own world class mega-city.

While a chorus of millionaire boosters, planning serfs, political hacks and media flaks mindlessly repeats "world class city" like a mantra, (recalling *The Simpsons* episode in which the whole town chants "monorail"), Vancouver has pursued one money-pit megaproject after another like Alice chasing the White Rabbit through some hallucinatory West Coast Wonderland. From Expo 86 to the 2010 Olympics, the city ran roughshod over concerns about socio-economic impact on the existing populace and environment while expanding the mandate of authorities like the GVRD and Translink in an apparent quest to become a West Coast version of Toronto—Canada's only certifiable mega-city and best example of the future of our cities if the conventional model of urban development prevails.

Vertical expansion (building higher) is theoretically supposed to discourage urban sprawl by delivering infrastructure more efficiently and economically. In fact, city skylines become aerial arenas where developers compete for views shrunk to slivers (remember *that* movie?) and increasingly consist of glimpses of other skyscrapers. Traditional planning solutions for problems of urban expansion seem about as effective as the rhythm method of birth control.

## Don't Go There

On March 8, 2007, the *Toronto Star* reported the acrimonious debate over Toronto's capital budget under the headline, "City decays as debt climbs." Just servicing a debt that ballooned from $1.4 billion to $2.3 billion, "will cost every Toronto household roughly $2,352 over the next five years," Councillor David Shiner groaned and, according to the *Star*, "The roads backlog alone is $300 million, but there's only $5 million budgeted for that purpose this year, down from $10 million last year." Bottom line: the cost of living in a Mega-City is going up and you'll be getting less for your money.

Example: in April 2007 *The Province*, reported that Vancouver city council cried "Uncle" after five years of arm-twisting by a local business group calling themselves the Vancouver Fair Tax Coalition. Council froze business property taxes for the year, forcing homeowners to fork over 8% more to make up the difference. Ed Des Roches, co-chairman of the coalition and VP of Plum Clothing commented, "I hope residents understand that business has subsidized them for many years—and also hope it will now motivate them to look much more carefully at how their dollars are spent."

Note the clumsy deflection of blame. Homeowners should worry about how *council* (mis)spends their tax money, not respond by declining to spend their disposable income, (reduced by 8%) at businesses like, say, Plum Clothing. Apparently it hasn't occurred to Ed that his customers might *really* look much more carefully at how their dollars are spent, decide to sell off their tax burdened homes and spend their windfall in some other town. In the short run, he might be right—the rich will bitch and raise rents on their revenue properties to cover the tax hike while the urban poor snarl, take it up the ass and become even more disenfranchised and vicious. Clock the increasing number of shootings in Toronto and Vancouver every year.

Vancouverites used to be satisfied with sending pictures of themselves smugly jogging past Stanley Park daffodils in mid-March to friends in Toronto, a city they love as a source of urban *schadenfreude* anecdotes to reinforce their own sense of superiority. However sluggish Vancouver's cross-town traffic, now officially slower than that of Los Angeles, or how gridlocked the ancient Lions Gate Bridge might be, what are these, compared to the existential stasis of the Don Parkway at rush hour? Planning analysts often blame Vancouver's traffic congestion on geography. Lack of any big city to the north or west meant no freeway bypass or flyover system was ever built. The Trans-Canada Highway simply dead-ended in Vancouver's crowded downtown eastside. The railroad stopped calling Vancouver "Terminal City" because it didn't exactly sound inviting, however true.

Trying to make a virtue of its come-lately urban infrastructure, Vancouver takes the line that not having citizens grovel in the shadow of elevated concrete expressways or pay admission to sit in the shade of a real tree makes it a candidate for the title of liveable, sustainable, *Postmodern* City of the Future. In some architectural circles, the business of 'revitalizing' downtown neighbourhoods by flogging $2000+-per-square-foot condos is actually being called *Vancouverization*. Yet an article by Charles Montgomery, entitled "Futureville," in the May/June 2006 issue of *Canadian Geographic* touting Vancouver as the new model of sustainable urban development, stirred up a shit-storm response from citizens and former residents.

In the subsequent issue, correspondent Gerald Dickie, manager of a large east end grain terminal, pointed out that the "obscene" tax burden of doing business and the cost of living in downtown Vancouver was driving both industrial suppliers and employees further out of the city, to the towns of the Fraser Valley: "I fully expect that I will have to retire elsewhere and that my children will not be able to afford to live here in the future. That, to me, is the real measure of whether Vancouver has achieved sustainability."

Former Vancouverite W. Robert Ballantyne snarled, "To join the happy throng of 80,000 people... doing what was once considered unthinkable: living in the downtown core,' one must be very, very wealthy. The headline on your cover would have more accurately read: 'Is Vancouver becoming the ideal sustainable city *for multi-millionaires?*" Bruce Beckler's graphic portrait of a dystopic downtown and his admission that he now "sleeps well through the night" in Surrey adds insult to injury, given *that* suburb's rep for stolen car chases, crack houses, and late night gang gunnery.

## The Albert Speer School of Architecture

No city passionately pursuing a quest, especially when the prize is wealth, power and global validation, wants to hear that they may be working from an out-of-date map, but this is what some architects and designers have been saying for almost two decades. The Fall 2002 issue of *Canadian Architect*, magazine of the Royal Architectural Institute of Canada, included a dispatch by Peter Yeadon reporting on the XXI World Congress of Architecture hosted by the *Union Internationale des Architects* in Berlin that summer. Berlin, Yeadon observed archly, was a popular venue with some delegates: "For University of Nevada historian Jane Ward, Berlin has become the new model for cities like Las Vegas to aspire to, as Berlin has achieved an exemplary pageantry of nostalgia, exoticism and futurism—the three main tenets of strip development."

Yeadon declined to ponder reasons Berlin might fail to challenge New York's claim to the title of "capital of the 20th century"— it's role as capital of the most infamous fascist state in a century replete with competitors, or as prostrate divided city, living symbol of forty years of Cold War between global superpowers, to suggest but two. Erasing the scars of its recent history was no doubt in the front of the reunified German mind when it spent the last decade of the century inviting international star architects and designers to re-create the city with an energy that would've gladdened the heart of Hitler's pet architect, Albert Speer, even as it offended his aesthetic sensibilities. Postmodern Germany's "zeal for rapid reunification was to focus on Berlin as the resuscitated *Hauptstadt*, the New Berlin," Yeadon noted, "From the beginning of unification, the entire nation rallied around the city as the representation of confidence and optimism, unity and plurality."

Plurality is the Postmodern urban grail. Canadians call it multiculturalism. It used to be called cosmopolitanism, achieved by cities like Rome, London and Paris after centuries of economic prosperity resulting from a *laissez-faire* inclusiveness, a tolerance for the many whose agendas of individual self-interest incidentally enhanced the power and prestige of the civic collective. Forcing it to bloom in a scant decade was a tall order, Yeadon admitted: "If the New Berlin was to represent diversity and excellence through architecture, it required bold contributions from world-renowned architects—those individuals I have called nextperts. We can now look back and scrutinize the offerings of this enormous international cast of architects and planners."

While the nextperts scrutinized, Berliners were already voting with their feet. Yeadon noted that "The *Berliner Zeitung* reported in July 2002 that more than 30,000 disenchanted Berliners traverse the city boundary every year, moving to parts unknown. The Prognos think tank speculated that 180,000 would leave Berlin by 2010."

## Not Leaving Las Vegas

Nextperts in Berlin may ascribe this *wanderlust* to the international drain of intellectual and financial elites to greener pastures, specifically the United States. Even so, their exit is hardly a ringing endorsement of "the new model for cities like Las Vegas to aspire to," since, unlike Berlin, Las Vegas is growing, due to the influx of predominantly Mexican-American workers needed to service the infrastructure of Byzantine casino entertainment complexes constructed over the last three decades. Its birth midwifed by Mob money—capitalism at its purest—the former dusty desert way-station was themed, however tackily, from the get go and has been repeatedly re-built with a speed and efficiency that must have modern architects, embarrassed by spectacular failures of architect-planned cities like Brasilia, slavering with envy.

From the 1950s on, Las Vegas grotesquely caricatured the "exemplary pageantry of nostalgia, exoticism and futurism," U. of Nevada

Prof. Jane Ward so admires in Berlin, and produced a product it could *sell* to the masses—the City-as-circus. With casinos now confected to mimic the ambiance of Paris, New York, even Venice, complete with canals on a *second* storey, Las Vegas has become the Sum of All Cities, the ultimate Postmodern Metropolis. Prefer Athens, Rome, or Beijing? They'll build a Parthenon, Coliseum and a Forbidden City next year on The Strip. Yet the notion that Las Vegas might serve as a model for any emergent mega-city or developing community is as ludicrous as it is appalling.

Berliners are not alone in their exodus from the post modern metropolis. In April 2007, Associated Press reported that demographic studies carried out by the Population Reference Bureau, a private research think-tank, indicate that *all* major American cities, other than the anomalies of Las Vegas and Atlanta, echo the Berlin flight-pattern. For the first time in their histories large American cities, including New York, are totally dependent on immigration just to maintain current population levels (i.e. their tax base), while populations of smaller towns are growing and their economies reviving.

Statistics Canada reports, "The initial results of the 2006 Census show that urbanization is continuing in Canada," an overall pattern of rural depopulation and urban growth consistent with the modern model. However, as Alan Broadbent admitted in an article for *The Walrus*, ("Brighter Lights, Bigger Cities," June 2006), there are enough people out there in the country that former PM Stephen Harper's "January 23, 2006, victory returned no seats from Vancouver, Toronto and Montreal." Broadbent, CEO of a capital investment corporation who beats the drum for Mega-polis like a Sally Ann evangelist, prophesied Harper's government would fall unless it developed policies that address the problems of Canada's major cities, yet every bit of evidence he cites is as useful to the prosecution as it is to the defence, starting with the above observation, which proves rural Canada still wields a big enough stick to elect a government without throwing a single bone to urban junkyard dogs.

Broadbent complained, "On average, urban ridings are represented by one Member of Parliament for just under 120,000 residents, while rural ridings get a federal representative for just over 86,000 people... As it stands, an urban vote is worth almost one-third less than a rural vote." Late in 2018, the B.C. provincial government held a referendum on electoral reform to redress this imbalance in favour of a scheme of proportional representation (more votes for urban dwellers) whose terms they neglected to define. There's a fine old English word for this kind of political Three-card Monte, re-jigging electoral boundaries to maximize the advantage of a party power-base—*gerrymandering*.

"Just give us a blank cheque and we'll fill in the amount behind closed doors and let you know," didn't play well with voters, sixty percent of whom told them to go fuck spiders. Rural electors, (the people who actually grow and raise the food city-dwellers eat) retain that slight advantage, some consolation for the life of indebtedness to urban-based banks who own the farm. Frankly, if simply moving to the boonies will give my vote more clout and spare this country another expensive, asinine constitutional crisis that does nothing but deepen our political cynicism, I'll put Ma and the kids in the wagon directly.

Anyone with an eye on the real estate market, (who hasn't?) knows Alan Broadbent is blowing Monte Cristo #10 smoke up his own Armani boxers. Formerly quiet backwaters of Canada—the Okanagan and Kootenay valleys, Vancouver Island, the Niagara peninsula, the Miramachi valley in New Brunswick, the towns of

Prince Edward Island—have all experienced a quiet renaissance as baby boomers flog their overpriced city properties to immigrants, pay off their mortgages and retire to more bucolic and affordable digs.

## It Takes a Village

At the 2002 Berlin conference Peter Yeadon also noted that a Canadian architect gave pro-urbanization delegates a swift kick in their PoMo backsides: "Unexpectedly, it was a Canadian scholar and architect who entertained one of the largest crowds at the Congress and delivered a paper that earnestly pursued this relationship between resources and resourcefulness. Richard Kroeker of Dalhousie University's School of Architecture, in a plenum on the architecture of 2030, turned the tables by stating that the architecture of the future was the architecture of villages."

Kroeker's call-to-disarm was comparatively muted. He merely cited examples of African villages that developed economically viable, environmentally friendly infrastructure solutions by using local ingenuity and technology, instead of depending on 'high-tech welfare' imported from the West, which often failed under local conditions and required long delays for replacement parts or repair. Some celebrity nextperts have already made more sweeping predictions about the shift from urban to village life. Most widely-quoted on the subject is American urbanist and community planner, Robert McIntyre. Quotes that follow come from the twenty-year anniversary issue of *Canadian House & Home* (Dec.2006), but have been repeated in many media. Like Yeadon, McIntyre credits himself with the invention of a cultural buzzword—a quicker route to fame than urbanics or community planning—in this case, *The New Village*.

"I coined the term to describe a type of rural land development with enough self-reliance to be classified and marketed as a traditional village," McIntyre says. "New Villages are inspired by the dispersed agricultural villages where your ancestors may have lived, but have been updated for the 21st century. For example, a typical New Village will create a diverse economy driven by the rapidly growing number of tele-workers and by the home-based businesses that are already common in rural areas." (This may explain why every rural property offered for sale in BC boasts a separate 220-volt wired, insulated workshop, unless the 'man-cave' thing has really gotten out of hand.)

McIntyre claims to have identified 5,700 places in Canada and the US, including ghost towns, that could qualify as initial bases of what amounts to a cultural revolution: "I decided that if a settlement has less than 1,000 residents and produces most of the jobs, food, water and energy within its boundaries, then the community qualifies as a New Village," McIntyre says, "This modest level of self-sufficiency avoids much of the air pollution, traffic congestion and other sprawl-related problems created by parasitic bedroom communities where transportation can account for half of the total energy use."

## Village of the Damned

The parameters of McIntyre's definition of the New Village have been narrowed for maximum media impact. There are tens of thousands of communities of more than 1,000 souls in North America whose economies are predominantly local and whose experience of the torments of urban sprawl is negligible. When we moved to Squamish in 1994, it had a population of 12,000, yet it still fit McIntyre's definition. Lapses of air quality were not due to the filter-stifled pulp mill, but to the number of residents who mitigated energy bills with traditional wood stoves. Traffic congestion resulted from the Squamish Double-Park—two drivers going opposite directions would just stop in the middle of the main drag to chat for five minutes. Other motorists waited politely for the conversation to finish. Nobody so much as tapped a horn. Road-rage was rude, not neighbourly, a sign you were some entitled Vancouver asshole on his way to Whistler.

Our water comes from the Seven Wells of Mashiter Creek. Minimally filtered, it gets chewy after heavy rains. I ignore Boil Water Advisories because it tastes like tap water in North Vancouver did, back when I grew up and Greater Vancouver was two-thirds less great. The town no longer produces its own food, but with an economy based on payrolls of the wood fibre pulp mill, the BC Rail shops and logging outfits of various sizes, Squamish could afford to sneer at tourist traffic on Highway 99. You still see bumper stickers from those days bearing an upraised middle finger and the salutation *Whistler is That Way*—a quaint gesture with which locals distinguished themselves from the entitled scum in the MacDonald's parking lot of a weekend.

Those stickers are now as faded as the *Forestry Feeds My Family* ones plastered beside them. The trucks are no longer new models. The first five years of the Millennium brought permanent closure of the mill, the sale of BC Rail to Chicago-owned CN with buyouts and layoffs at the rail-yards and the steady decline of logging—all spikes in the coffin of local independence. Led by Mayors and councils eager to kiss the assets of any developer with two slabs of beaverboard to rub together, the town lavished millions on a highway-side Adventure Centre U-Nev. Prof Jane Ward would love, since it combines nostalgic timber-frame joinery with the naïve futurism of *The Jetsons* and early 1960s drive-in burger joints.

The town frantically reinvented itself as *Canada's Outdoor Recreation Capital*. Municipal signs now direct visitors to world famous wind-surfing at the Spit and climbing on the Stawamus Chief—the same visitors former councils disparaged only a few years before as 'hippies who live in vans and contribute nothing to the local economy.' Squamish no more fits any stretch of McIntyre's vision of a 'village' than does Whistler, its tourist-dependent nemesis to the north, which has become a cash-cow whose jugular the province needs to regularly tap for sustaining life-blood without killing the beast.

As for the African proverb, "It takes a village to raise a child," the plague of fentanyl, Xanax and crystal meth use and violent crime among our kids suggests that as modern villagers, we're no better than the urban rich for whose awful offspring Whistler has become Fort Lauderdale North; a place without consequences. Whistler witlessly plagiarized a Las Vegas marketing slogan inviting irresponsible hedonism—"*What happens in Whistler stays in Whistler*"—and now whines when visitors take them up on it and trash the town. Old and young, many Squamish residents are cashing in their Olympic Highway equity bonus and lighting out for places like Powell River, Enderby, Lumby, Salmon Arm, Grand Forks, joining the worldwide club of runaways from the postmodern urban nightmare, looking for a Global Village of their dreams.

## New Village People

The difference between McIntyre's idealized New Villagers and the equally idealized traditional swain and milkmaid is that the New Villager is educated, electronically-enabled and financially independent, or nearly so, thanks to equity acquired by exiting some urban Sodom or Gomorrah without looking back except on 250 channel cable TV and broadband high-speed internet. They are not the rich, for as critics of Charles Montgomery's "Futureville" article noted, even a dysfunctional modern city is a fine place to live if money is no object. New Villagers are the ex-urban, ex-middle class; sick of traffic, crime, stress, watching their children turn into drugged video droogs and their nest egg for the future devoured by a predatory cost of living.

They are also *older*. Despite a back-wash of disaffected urban escapees, Statistics Canada's 2006 Census reports: "In all metropolitan areas combined, more than one person in three (35.7%) was between twenty and forty-four years of age in 2006, a much higher proportion than in rural areas, where young adults made up only 27.7% of the population. The difference is primarily due to internal migration of young adults, who often leave rural areas in their late teens and early twenties to pursue their education or to find a job in urban areas."

In prose that makes Trojan prophetess Cassandra sound like a TV weather-girl, StatsCan notes, "rural areas also have a higher proportion of people aged sixty-five and over, and that proportion is growing faster than in urban areas", daring to suggest that "With fewer young, working-age adults, more seniors and more rapid population aging, rural areas may encounter some challenges in meeting the needs of an older population, for example, in the area of health and home-care services. These challenges may increase in the near future, when the first baby-boomers turn sixty-five years." No shit, Sherlock.

There's a reason these drones work for StatsCan instead of in the public sector. The post-WWII baby boom age-wave has been the biggest marketing opportunity in modern history. Anyone who catches that curl rides it to riches. Twenty years ago my brother-in-law and I saw gated communities of ranch style (no stairs/wheelchair accessible) homes being built in Kelowna. He said, "We should buy a drugstore and a couple of cheap Hondas and offer free home delivery of prescriptions. Later, we'll move into the funeral home racket." If we had, I wouldn't be writing this. I'd be too busy counting money.

Despite their professed desire for the simple charms of small town life, when middle-class boomers become New Villagers they'll take their demand for goods and full services with them. If you're old, blind or confused, the government can rescind your driver's license, but they can't take away your right to *buy*—or to vote. We haven't really begun to see how Grey Power will reshape our country and culture, but you can be sure of one thing: somebody is going to make a hell of a lot of money off it. The question is, *who*?

## Village Voices

In a June 27, 2007 interview as frank as a political suicide note, B.C. Housing Minister Rich Coleman disparaged the ribbon-cutting photo-op policies preferred by politicians faced with urban social problems and dared to call a ground-breaking spade a fucking shovel. According to the *Vancouver Province*, Coleman bluntly stated, "the eventual answer for the homeless of Vancouver's Downtown Eastside is relocation—to another B.C. community. The Downtown Eastside is going to have to change. Over time, it frankly needs to disperse its problems out of that one particular area of the city. We can't put all the services for these folks in one place, because we're creating our own self-fulfilling prophecy."

So much for cost-effective centralization of services. Ordinarily, I'd interpret an inclination to agree with a representative of any provincial government as reason to speed-dial the Mental Health crisis-line. Yet Coleman is the only Housing Minister, (including those under NDP governments), who has actually offered much in the way of *practical* help to residents of the Downtown Eastside. His government ponied-up $37 million to buy up ten single-room-occupancy hotels on the Downtown Eastside to prevent almost 600 rooms from being 'gentrified' as condos or turned into fleabag hostels by landlords greedy to wring a jackpot out of the 2010 Olympics. His government jacked the welfare rate by $100 a month and the shelter allowance by $50, dropped $11 million into the Salvation Army tambourine to support Grace Mansion's work with eighty-five high risk residents on East Hastings, provided funding for emergency shelters at churches in the area during the winter and worked with the city of Vancouver to develop 300 new social housing units on city-owned sites.

East End housing activists were guardedly grateful, but more suspicious of Coleman's gift horse than the Trojans—with good cause. Coleman's rhetoric recalled euphemisms about "emigration to the east" once used by Nazi officials to describe cattle-car excursions whose final destinations were not resort villages. The Liberals made no secret of their desire to see Vancouver turned into a "Futureville" of modernist monoliths co-existing with gutted heritage facades in a multi-cultural pageantry of "nostalgia, exoticism and futurism"; a pluralist hive of happy condo-dwellers and mall-shoppers with 1/26$^{th}$ ownerships in Whistler time-shares—a *polis* fit to welcome the world in 2010.

"Towns in the Fraser Valley and the Interior offer a better chance at an escape from the addiction cycle that leads to homelessness,"

Coleman insisted, threatening that, "communities who object to taking in those now gravitating overwhelmingly to Vancouver's streets will get little of his sympathy if they try to keep the poor and troubled from their midst."

Even if this was just a cheap political ploy to disperse Vancouver's homeless, criminal and mentally-ill street people into the hinterland so they won't embarrass the Liberals or the City of Vancouver in 2010, what if he was *right*, albeit for the wrong reasons?

However legitimate their immediate concerns, for decades activists like the Downtown Eastside Residents Association, (DERA) have fought a rear-guard action against the gentrification that disenfranchises the working poor without ever once answering the larger question—*why* fight for the right to continue living in what is officially admitted to be one of the worst urban shit-holes in all of Canada?

## Redeveloping the Deserted Village

Oliver Goldsmith's "The Deserted Village" is a classic Romantic eulogy for rural English culture destroyed as country folk were lured from healthy hamlets to pestilential urban slums of the early Industrial Revolution by the illusion of economic advantage. The plagues have changed, but prospects for today's urban poor are still low-paid futureless jobs, an ugly toxic environment and a social milieu that corrupts from kindergarten. No one disputes that country life is healthier, less stressful, environmentally friendlier and more socially supportive than life in the metropolitan gutter, where the poor are doomed to be 'outsiders-looking-in' through plate-glass restaurant and boutique windows at a lifestyle systemically denied to them.

In small towns, someone with 'chronic substance abuse issues' gets handled more like Otis the town drunk from *Mayberry RFD* than downtown road-kill. In Squamish, RCMP members still know the personal and family histories of 'frequent flyers' and the threat-level they represent. If you don't present as the Stranger Who Might Kill Me, police officers treat you with tolerance and respect, which means there's less risk of getting your ticket punched every time you get a little over-stimulated.

Rent or mortgage payment, the biggest bite out of any pay cheque is smaller in small towns. Even gas is usually cheaper, since adding a penny a litre in Greater Vancouver is more profitable than kicking the price a full nickel in small towns, despite the higher transport cost. All this, *and* your vote is worth $1/3^{rd}$ more? So why doesn't the whole population of Vancouver's downtown eastside book it down to the bus station and ride the Hound upcountry to any one of a thousand small towns tomorrow?

For the same reasons more than half the world's total population have migrated to large cities, either in their own countries or in others. Following the mirage of greater opportunities, immigrants invariably settle in large cities, accept lousy jobs and often suffer discrimination in exchange for finding ready-made communities of their own culture. One of the blind spots of government agencies at every level is the failure to recognize the urban poor as a distinct community whose solidarity crosses even obvious racial lines. The best novels to come out of Vancouver's Downtown Eastside are Peter Trower's *Dead Man's Ticket* and Joe Ferone's *Boomboom*. Though set thirty years apart, characters in both novels are trapped in tragic fates by their inability to leave The Block, to just hop a cross-town bus to Marpole or the North Shore, or Ride the Hound to Williams Lake, Nakusp or Chetwynd, *anywhere*, and start a new life. Like a dysfunctional family, a dysfunctional community is better than none and the demons you know seem preferable to their District Manager.

If city and provincial politicians want Vancouver's downtown rounders and new immigrants to move to Princeton or Dawson Creek, and if any federal politician wants to turn the tide of young people abandoning the country for the city, they need to do two things: 1) Recognize the economic opportunities presented by baby-boomers moving to small towns, (which they'll do or get voted out), and 2) Reverse the policies of centralizing education and essential services, like health care, which they have manipulated to extirpate unique village cultures—Newfoundland's outports being the first example—over the past five decades. Policies like the plan to replace unionized health care workers in the Okanagan with low-paid contract workers are not the way to attract new villagers to Interior towns. If they want to make New Villagers out of Vancouver's urban poor, politicians need to buy steel-toed work boots, storm into to the offices of cabinet toadies and stomp some serious rump. Then put those boots to private sector hogs like certain charter banks that cut costs by closing small town branches, leaving ATMs to collect service fees without actually providing any services other than a touch-pad.

## Global Village Idiots

Long before Robert MacIntyre coined the concept of the New Village, culture critics like Jane Jacobs, (*The Death and Life of Great American Cities*) and planner/statistician Anthony Downs, whose *Stuck in Traffic* grimly concludes that the number of vehicles will always expand to fill the available asphalt, abandoned the modern metropolis as a workable social construct. Whether or not we recognize it, their conclusion that most urban problems are ultimately insoluble is a tipping point in our cultural evolution. These aren't "back to the land" neo-Luddite hippies running off to get naked in a bush commune. They're serious smart people who see Canadian media savant Marshall McLuhan's vision of the Global Village as the only possible future for mankind.

When McLuhan coined the term more than five decades ago, he imagined a future in which interactive mass media would unite all citizens of the planet, urban and rural, in the cozy intimacy of a *village*. He didn't call it the Global City or the Global Suburb. He knew cities weren't going to disappear. Cities developed at crossroads of caravan routes, on estuaries and inlets that offered sheltered anchorage for cost-effective maritime commerce, and later on the flat *tabula rasa* of the North America prairies or Russian steppes, where their locations were determined by the logistical needs of railroads. Neither of these communication systems is obsolete. Amazon can't teleport goods over the internet yet. More than 90% of the world's major commercial cargo and mail still moves by economical ship and rail, not by air.

Prosperity empowered cities to become centres of patronage for the arts and sciences, especially architects, whose discipline is a combination of both. Urban wealth and power directly resulted from the real estate mantra, "location, location, location." It was economically essential for cities to attract workers, financial brokers, bankers and service industry hucksters always ready to skim a crowd. In the 1960s, McLuhan recognized that masses of city-dwelling industrial workers were being made redundant by mechanization and electronic technology would make it possible for financial and information services to be located anywhere. CIBC could move it's corporate head office to Nakusp if it wanted to. Ever-expanding cities have simply become a human bad habit, like smoking—something we do even though we know it's unhealthy and that fresh country air tastes better without a filter-tip.

Despite its pretentious Upper Class Twit of the Year tone, *Country Life* remains one of Britain's most popular magazines, subscribed to by economic aristocrats who only visit their country houses on weekends but actually read by those who dream of joining their class. The sprawling suburbs of North American cities were inspired by this traditional English idealization of 'country life.' The New World couldn't promise Everyman a castle, but it had space to make him a squire, lord of a conspicuously useless front lawn once reserved for rural manors, and master of a barbecue where he could display his sophistication by immolating self-consciously 'rustic' meals on a patio altar. This yearning for the even lamest illusions of rural life is so powerful that while cities like Vancouver try to re-invent the vision of cosmopolitan of downtown living, their suburbs continue to spread like fibrous tumours.

McLuhan failed to anticipate that ownership of mass media, including internet service providers, would become concentrated in the hands of ad-revenue driven trans-national conglomerates that would re-develop his global village into a planetary strip mall where we all still owe our souls to a company store that sells the same shit under a variety of local banners. He also failed to foresee the emergence of an underclass of global village idiots, disenfranchised because they're unable to afford personal computers, iPods, XBoxes and iPhones, just as he'd be shocked to see articles in contemporary magazines chronicling the agonies of those so wired-in they're melting down under the stress of information overload.

In his enthusiasm for the virtual village, McLuhan overlooked the enduring power of the real one, home of what Brian Fawcett, Canada's foremost culture critic since Big Mc, calls the 'local and authentic'—the deep impact of *real* geography, climate, economics and history on the community and culture it produces. Whatever the socio-economic makeup of New Villagers, their only hope of creating a viable social alternative to the nihilistic hedonism and fluffy futurist consumerism of urban real estate brochures is to grasp the meaning of the ancient Taoist saying, "Truth resides in the hearth"—in the thousands of small domestic interactions with family and neighbours that make up everyday life in an authentic community.

Sprawled on the moss-riddled lawn of my now million-dollar Squamish split-level tract house at night, I squint to glimpse stars that once flooded the grass with a light so ethereal Mary and I tore off our clothes to conceive one of our children under it. Now those stars are dimmed by the glare of twenty-four hour arc lights illuminating parking lots big enough to host tank battles just down the hill. In my head I hear a refrain from an old Bob Dylan song that seems to have acquired a sharper edge.

*And you ask why I don't live here?*
*Honey, how come you don't MOVE?*

TWO

# A Walk on the Wild Side

When Mary and I bought a house in Squamish in the 1990s, three people I worked with immediately hit on me about my garage, seeking storage for wind-surfboards, hang-gliders and kayaks. Plus the guy who asked if he could park a trailer with twin Ski-Doos in my side yard under a tarp. They all lived in apartments in downtown Vancouver.

"Why did you buy these damn toys if you have no place to keep them?" I felt like screaming, but I already knew the answer because back then I was scratching a living by writing outdoor adventure features for local periodicals. They bought the damn things so that for one or two days of the week they could play at being someone who doesn't live in a 500 square foot shoebox in the claustrophobic density of Vancouver's West End or Yaletown, while still being able to drive their Stupid Unnecessary Vehicles back from Whistler in time to make the scene at some bistro in mud-spattered togs for a round of crantinis and pre-dinner bragging.

Small companies had begun offering guided "wilderness experiences" that combined physical challenges with a supposedly nonintrusive, more spiritual experience of the natural world. Mostly run by people trying to make a living doing what they loved, they were usually happy to take a journalist along in exchange for the publicity value of an editorial feature—about ten times more effective than a paid advertisement of equivalent size none of them could afford. I bluffed my way into sea-kayaking, rock climbing, paragliding, rafting river rapids, mountain biking, avalanche survival and winter camping courses, the whole bag. Often I was treated to lunch and more beer than was good for me. Then I got paid to write about my experiences. For a writer, this is as good as it gets.

Time is a D-8 Cat that scrapes away the vacant lot where you played baseball and flattens the woods where you built your tree fort. A scant dozen years later, even the wisdom of turning wilderness areas into adventure theme parks for weekend warriors and tourists to defray the cost of their preservation already seemed problematic. We're more aware that any kind of development shrinks the planet and the so-called eco-tourism and adventure tourism industries have turned out to be fraternal rather than identical twins, with very different agendas.

Eco-tourism purists object to snowmobiles and ATVs spewing gasoline fumes and wildlife-spooking noise into the pure wilderness they've promised clients. They deplore the harassment of cetacean mammals by powerboats over-laden with seasick whale voyeurs spewing vegan lunches into the pristine waters. The wider and more boisterous adventure tourism fraternity, which has spun off whole sub-genres of Xtreme Sports, sees these criticisms as party-pooping and maintains that getting people out into the wilderness by any means is justified by the end of making them more sensitive to the plight of embattled Nature.

This Jacob and Esau cage-match will probably be a headliner for decades to come, but despite its internecine tensions, the outdoor recreation industry and its Xtreme Sports spin-offs have clearly caused a fundamental paradigm shift in our culture. The Post-Modern zeitgeist has caught up with sport. The modern age of the passive-ironic disinterested spectator in both the arts and popular culture is over: we have become a culture of participants.

## "Just Do It"—NIKE slogan from the 1990s

Nowhere is that shift more apparent than in the only global cultural event our species has managed to produce: the *modern* Olympic Games. I stress the word *modern* because when the Olympics were revived in late 19th century Europe, we'd already become an industrialized urban culture of spectators. In his history of leisure time, *Waiting for the Weekend* (Viking 1991), McGill University architecture professor and culture critic Witold Rybczynski observes that the shift to corporate-sponsored team sports played by professional athletes actually occurred a century earlier, led by pub owners who noticed they sold more ale and pies when the local farm boys got up a game of cricket on the village green. In no time, players were put on the payrolls of breweries, the green fenced on game days and admission charged. Sport became something you watched while consuming large quantities of beer and junk food. *Plus ça change…*

Watching the 2006 Winter Olympic Games on TV, (lager and Cheezy-Poofs at hand) I had to wonder if the whole Olympic Idea might be on the verge of core-level marketing failure. Except for a few moments, like when a freestyler shot his bindings on a jump and nailed his landing *without skis*, or when the Netherlands bobsled pair took the bottom half of the run upside down, the Turin Olympics seemed, well, let's be honest, just plain dull.

Seeing a bunch of people 'race' on cross-country skis or skates—not even allowed to thump or trip each other like *Rollergirls*—can't help but underwhelm TV viewers accustomed to watching people with double-digit IQs drive ATVs off sheer cliffs or try to jump bikes to the top of apartment buildings from homemade plywood ramps on Reality TV programs like the Max X List, never mind the sadistic stunts contrived by *Fear Factor*. Who wants to watch a pair of girls in modest *maillots* do synchronized swimming once you've seen a 42D-cup bimbo in a Malibu bikini, (or some buff young stud in a Speedo), undo padlocks underwater in a clear plastic tank filled with giant pinching crabs for a $50,000 jackpot?

The real problem with all Olympic events isn't their lack of appeal to cathode-lobotomized sofa lizards. They're no longer a dominant majority. For the first time in history since the Classical Age, many of the people who make up the audience for the Games are themselves weekend warriors; amateur athletes who regularly engage in Xtreme Sports that that would give a pampered Olympian the yellow squirts. If you spend your weekends paragliding, base-jumping, wind-surfing, ice-climbing or riding a bike down steep mountain trails at top speed, you're bound to feel a bit *blasé* watching some coddled "star" flit down a pre-set engineered course to a victory measured in hundredths of a second.

## Adrenaline Junkies

As kids, we do things our parents warn us against to define ourselves as individuals, chicks who no longer cower in the nest waiting for

Mom and Dad to hork up pre-digested social values. For my post-WWII generation who came of age in the 1960s, this took the form of risky politics, risky drugs and risky sex. The acid test of any form of rebellion is whether or not it gives you what psycho-neurologists try to quantify as an endorphin/adrenaline high—the feeling you got when you climbed to the top of the forbidden cherry tree, rode your bike no-hands down the steepest hill in the neighbourhood, or played knock-on-ginger on the meanest old man on the block and he chased you with a flashlight and a nine-iron.

The sand pit was a place we were absolutely forbidden to play, a big semi-circular hole dug out of the side of a ridge near Cleveland Dam in North Vancouver. From up in the hot resinous shadows of the scrub firs, it was about five times higher than the roof of your house, as kids measure. The trick was seeing that halfway down long slopes of pure soft sand would break your fall, cushioning your slide to the bottom. You just needed the jam to take that first screaming step off the edge to slide down to glory and shake a bucket of grit out of your jeans. Today's guided adventures and X-treme sports depend on the courage to take that step, to launch yourself out the door of the plane at 10,000 feet, turn your kayak or canoe into white-water, stretch for the hand-hold that gets you around the overhang, stay on your bike when the trail dives down a shale slope of plus forty-five degrees. Make one split-second decision to hang in and the rest is reflex, will to survive and the perversity to brag about seriously hurting yourself when you do.

The adrenaline rush of fear, then relief, is a high-colonic for the brain. Portrayal of this kind of risk-taking as a healthy, active lifestyle masks the discovery that adrenaline and endorphins appear to be the body's natural cocaine and heroin speedball—improving performance, blunting pain and inducing delusions of invulnerability. Like all good things, this enzyme junk is addictive, even potentially lethal. It can also lead to Reality TV madness like the annual international Eco-Challenge race, in which teams of annoying over-achievers from around the world pay obscene amounts of money to whine about undergoing the kind of hardships that in wartime would result in atrocity trials.

Nostalgia for the euphoria of risk has become a billion dollar industry. Every time we Baby Boomers roll over in bed, some clever dick invents a new technologically-enhanced mattress and makes a bundle to stick under it simply because there's so many of us with so much money that even a moderate market share of any product sector translates into mass sales.

When our parents hit their forties, they accepted middle age gracefully, taking up low-impact social sports like curling and golf, which involve a lot of innocent fibbing in plush cocktail lounges. They adopted cardigan sweaters and elastic-waist slacks and skirts that looked vaguely sporty while taking into account the natural state of the human body in its pre-senile phase. Not us, man. Maybe we did transfer out of that creative ceramics major into an MBA program, or drop out and write the Securities & Exchange Commission exam to become a real estate agent or stockbroker. That doesn't mean we sold out. When some Jurassic rock radio station plays The Who's "My Generation" we crank up the sound system in the Volvo and screech along, "Hope I die before I get old!"

So when we find ourselves still alive and looking five-oh in the mirror, we won't abide any polyester polo-necked golf shirts or Sansabelt slacks in our walk-in closets—bigger than family apartments in some parts of the world. We're jogging, running marathons, triathlons, mountain biking, rock-climbing, para-sailing, spelunking and deep-sea diving, white-water or sea kayaking, cross-country skiing—anything that will give us back the adrenaline rush of youth our generation assumes is an inalienable human right—and our closets and storage lockers are stuffed with the over-priced gear to prove it.

Most X-sports require physical courage with no moral or political commitment. They're the natural organic version of the vicious sex, dangerous drugs and hedonistic head-banger music of the late 1970s, and the money and gluttony worship of the odious Decade of Greed that followed. We're fitter and we get more fresh air, but it's still just all about us having fun.

## Weekend Warriors

Outdoor adventure tourism and X-treme Sports bridge what was called, in our wild youth, the generation gap. Not just a Boomer fad, they're hugely popular with young people who still set the cultural tone and now even have their own X Games. X-sports are the participatory physical incarnation of Post-Modernism: they embody the Now, the instant of being intensely alive in the moment. Adopting the Post-Modern aesthetic of playful radical juxtaposition, they're creating new activities by taking techniques or pieces of equipment originally designed for one purpose and adapting it to another.

Ponder the reincarnation of the bicycle as an all-terrain vehicle. Invented in the late 19th century, it was a mechanical pony intended to reduce the vast daily tonnage of horse-shit that fouled city streets and water systems at a time when automobiles were still hand-built toys of the rich. A contraption designed for paved or graded roads, it was a cheap, clean mode of urban transportation. When bikes began re-appearing in traffic as ecologically-sound rides, I approved in principle, but as a hiker and dog walker, I was appalled when they left pavement. Bikes may be eco-friendly in the city, but in the woods they rapidly degrade trails, creating mud-wallows in the low spots and eroding the edges.

Mountain bikers also had serious attitude problems where safety and courtesy were concerned. In lower Mosquito Creek where I used to walk my dog, I was nearly de-gendered by a spandex-ed biker hurtling out of the salmonberries. I caught his handlebars just in time to stop him from giving me a free vasectomy and dumped him in the brambles accompanied by some strong language. As I stalked off, ignoring his attempted apology, he recovered enough to shout, "By the way, I'm *not* an asshole." Chain leash wrapped around my fist, I offered to introduce him to the concept of obedience training. White-faced, he remounted and pedalled off, no doubt convinced he'd encountered one of the mentally ill our Provincial government had recently expelled from supervised care facilities in order to save young urban stooges enough tax money to spend $5000 on bicycles.

Wind-surfboards gave the traditional Hawaiian sport, which went global as a subculture in the 1960s, new life by marrying it to quick-response sailing that is still a tradition in coastal Europe. The latest twist is kite boarding, which combines a small para-glider wing with a snowboard-length surfboard to maximize the aerial and aquatic thrill factors. As for a sport like street-luge—putting wheels on the one-man bobsled to run downhill races on pavement—first time I saw this on TV I instantly recalled the kamikaze crates we used to rig from a single plank, two-by-four axles, wheels pried off a stolen shopping-cart and a short rope for steering. Frills like soapbox coachwork and brakes were overlooked in our haste to launch down hills, praying posted lookouts were sharp-eyed and none of the wheels would fall off. Just to survive with nothing more than bruises and the loss of a few yards of skin made you feel like an indestructible superhero.

Enhanced by contemporary materials like Kevlar, the ancient Inuit kayak is an ideal craft for up-close exploring and low-impact adventuring in coastal waters. An Inuit hunter might approve of new sea kayaks on the basis of improved materials, but the idea of running any kayak down river rapids would strike him as typically insane white man behaviour. Rivers are full of rocks. Discovering them at high speed, upside down, when you're busy drowning, may detract from your appreciation of a newfound intimacy with the riparian environment.

True mother of all X-sports is the parachute. Invented in World War I to give pilots and balloon observers a marginal chance of survival, it was later used to drop spies and troops behind enemy lines. Those pilots and paratroopers would never have imagined that by the end of the 20th century people would *pay* to jump out of planes and deliberately prolong free-fall to do mid-air stunts— including riding and flipping on snowboards, a sort of air-surfing that may be the ultimate Po-Mo sport.

## The Illusion of Competence

Even traditional conservative recreational activities like mountaineering have been transformed by the Postmodern zeitgeist. Originally practice activities for the final acts of mountaineering, rock-climbing and bouldering detached themselves and became a separate sport during the latter half of the 20th century in the North American southwest, where Dali-esque rock formations and monotonously fine weather free the body from bulky clothing and packs so climbers can push the possibilities of pure technique to the limit.

There's nothing especially Postmodern about a specialist skill-set becoming a separate sport. What is supremely Po-Mo is the increasing number of climbers who learn their basic skills indoors, in climbing gyms that began to appear in North America in the early 1990s. Goofing on artificial walls, top-roped for safety with Pink Floyd's *Dark Side of The Moon* booming out of monster speakers may be a blast, but it doesn't prepare you for real rock that turns cold and slick when the weather changes, numbing your fingers after a few moves, or the brain-poaching effects of the sun if you start a pitch at the wrong time of day. Or horseflies that chow down on your calves when an instinctive slap at them will cost you your hold and possibly your life.

When I took a rock climbing course on the Smoke Bluffs in Squamish, the instructor turned up with a couple of ropes, slings and a handful of hardware he casually tossed on the ground. His modest gear cache did not impress a couple in their early forties, clad from neck to ankle in matching superhero lycra. The guy in particular kept casting covetous glances at young rock-rats on neighbouring pitches whose chests were criss-crossed with Rambo bandoliers dangling every nut, chock and widget in the catalogue. I made a point of asking, in front of everyone, "Does all that stuff really help?"

"It helps keep Mountain Equipment Co-op in business," the instructor answered with a smirk, provoking a scowl from the guy who'd been coveting the big racks. "Specialized gear is only useful if you already possess excellent basic climbing fundamentals.

If you don't, having all that stuff is actually dangerous. It gives you too much to think about and it can make you think you're a better climber than you are. That's how you get hurt."

In the Postmodern century, we no longer sell things on the basis that they make you look rich enough to *afford* them. We sell things, from cars to computers to sports gear, on the premise that they make you appear *competent* to use them. Replacing the image of wealth as the dominant status mode of our culture, the image of competence socially disenfranchises those who acquire wealth merely by the windfall of inheritance, luck or even the kind of acquisitive drive worshipped during the 1980s. Thorstein Veblen, the early 20th century economist who coined the term "conspicuous consumption" to explain the need of the rich to be seen to be so, would understand the necessity of buying $250 trail shoes to go for a walk in the park. But buying the image of competence, as opposed to mere wealth, opens a sack of mad rats.

Competence is harder to fake than wealth. Just buying top of the line gear won't cut it. You have to know how to use it, or look like a horse's ass. And no matter how odious I personally find some X-sports, it's obvious that learning the skills and participating in these activities can have life-transforming effects for large numbers of people, regardless of income. This makes them much more inclusive than the passive supposed solidarity of a whole nation watching televised Olympic events restricted to an elite of athletic champions. This paradigm shift is one of the eccentric shortcuts by which something resembling 'progress' in human culture occurs.

## The Global Hostel

Adventure tourism and X-sports have morphed into more than

recreational activities. Like the hippie movement of the 1960s, they are a form of non-confrontational social revolution for a culture so terminally disgusted with traditional politics that "taking it to the streets" now means grinding bikes and skateboards or doing free-form gymnastics off public structures (parkour) and "dropping out" entails an abrupt loss of real altitude.

In the 19th century, mountaineering was a subculture of eccentric amateurs, some inherently rich, others not so much, who spent every free moment among the cliffs, crags and snows. Many devotees still climb in that spirit, taking low-paying jobs in the hospitality industry, whose skills are portable, and work as little as they need to, enabling them to travel from Squamish to Joshua Tree, to the Dolomites, wherever there's steep rock and fresh challenges. Like the so-called surf bums who follow the sun around the world or ski bums who follow the snow, they're actually more than a bunch of drop-outs marginalized by a passion for a particular physical activity.

Today's eco/adventure tourism and X-sports destinations are the moveable *gymnasia* of the global village, places where the young and quick meet kindred spirits, some old and wise, from all over the world, making social and philosophical connections, spawning sub-cultures with networks that may possibly be models for future supra-national societies. We ought to be grateful for these signs of sanity in a younger generation, instead of whining because they're too smart to be loyal to corporate employers who treat them as members of an untouchable caste on principle.

Our society too often evaluates cultural phenomena on a balance sheet, but even in those terms it's obvious that outdoor adventure recreation generates far greater long-term economic benefits than any number of Olympic blowouts. Proliferating variations of Postmodern sports are all characterized by the investment of large amounts of money in lessons, specialized equipment and branded clothing that identifies the user as blessed with the status of a high disposable income as well as that of a supposedly serious athlete and adventurer. Add on the entrepreneurial opportunities for niche-market services like instruction and guiding, the manufacture of clothing and gear, factor in the travel and tourism spin-offs and you've got an industry. Not a closely held, hierarchical, traditional heavy industry, but possibly the new business model of a social revolution these sub-cultures are quietly engendering.

Some forward-looking nations, (Belize and Costa Rica, for instance), have staked their economic future on guided eco/adventure tours and X-sports, mainly because of their minimal environmental impact. Even the most egregious of these activities remain things post-Millennial yuppies do on weekends—things that don't take you too far from an ATM and a good restaurant. Since those engaged in them don't penetrate wilderness areas permanently or to any significant depth, the worst damage they do is the equivalent of dog-earing the pages of a library book.

Cranky purists, (don't look at me like that) may question the authenticity of the experiences offered by eco/adventure tourism. As a survivor of a wide random sampling, I have to admit these experiences are no more authentic than the guided African safaris of the 1950s written up by Ernest Hemingway and Robert Ruark. But authenticity is frequently a reactionary concept that appeals to an idealized past, a supposed golden age that usually proves to be more fabulous than fact.

When Hemingway and Ruark were affirming their manhood at the expense of big animals on the African veldt, they may not even have been aware that their Great White Hunter and native guides were discreetly covering them in accordance with Rule One of the adventure tourism industry: *Don't Let the Client Get Killed*. The Africa they described was a beautiful fiction of magnificent beasts and noble savages—a place that existed only in their writing, Hollywood films and the animatronic riverboat ride attraction at Walt Disney's first theme park. The real Africa of their time was still the continent-sized slave labour camp, perpetuated by febrile colonial administrations and global economic factors, it had been long before the term Third World was coined.

*That* was the story a generation of writers completely missed and it's a cautionary reminder that writing can be wonderful even when it's unintentionally describing a creature by looking at the wrong end. When a friend read my breathless article about spending a couple of winter nights in an emergency shelter I'd built out of snow, he sent me a copy of Ernest Shackleton's excruciating saga of survival after the failure of his Antarctic expedition. Humbled, I took his point. With appropriate Postmodern irony, guided adventures and X-sports do often trivialize the original activity that inspired them. White-water rafting and kayaking turn the death-defying river voyages of explorers like Simon Fraser and Alexander Mackenzie into jolly day-trip outings to scenic water-park attractions.

Is it fair and reasonable to evaluate these experiences against a revisionist and possibly fictional notion of authenticity? Every human experience is unique to its time and place and thus authentic in a sense. If somebody rides down the Thompson River rapids in a guided raft on an inane corporate team-building outing and has a life-changing experience, should we dismiss it because they weren't in brigade canoe paddled by indentured, toque-wearing suicidal voyageurs? Surely it's the result that counts, the long-term effect on human beings and the way they see themselves in relation to their own culture.

The *gratuitous* aspect of X-treme sports, their Postmodern self-conscious novelty, makes them fun to watch, even fun to try, but don't expect many of them to become Olympic events. The inclusion of snowboarding in the Olympics in the 1990s was a cynical marketing attempt to appeal to a younger generation who think the discus competition is some kind of lame Frisbee event. But while the playful silliness of most X-sports may mark their cards as ephemeral fads, by the time the International Olympic Committee gets around to even considering them, whole subcultures of weekend warriors will be long gone, off to some global adventure play park or *doing* something else, instead of *watching* the Olympics.

THREE

# Imaginary Geography

"Where's your house?"

This question preceded the exchange of names and possibly blows when we caught new kids poaching our huckleberries in the log-strewn vacant lots or exploring the fir-scented shells of half-framed houses. In the fall of 1960, we moved into a North Vancouver neighbourhood that existed mostly as a legal description in the District office. Our street had an improbable Spanish name stamped out in black letters on a white metal banner riveted to a steel pole. It lacked pavement, sidewalks, streetlights and, on our block, other houses. Since the word *neighbourhood* implies neighbours, we were stretching the definition.

Ours was one of many expansions of the Capilano Highlands, an area of former Crown land ceded to the District and subdivided at what was then no doubt the same obscene profit percentage enjoyed by developers today, a connivance of contractors and District officials who happily foresaw a day they when they'd be flogging view lots on the peaks of the North Shore mountains. From the look of the North Shore skyline today, they might get there yet.

Just below Skyline Drive, which led to the bottom of the old Grouse Mountain chairlift, our lots had barely been scraped out of the bush with a bulldozer. The aroma of fresh cut cedar spiced the air. Our stump-lined street looked more like a side-hill logging show than a suburb. Our neighbours were deer, coyotes, cougars and bewildered bears, who woke from hibernation to find brand new post-and-beam houses squatting on what used to be their salmonberry patches.

Wild animals outnumbered the human inhabitants of the few other houses, one or two on each new block, with whom we became acquainted by the default of necessity. The Universal Law of Neighbourhoods: neighbours are closer than in-laws. You're not related to them, even by marriage, but you're stuck with them—not just on big family occasions but every damn day. You live together as a kind of tribe.

## Birth of a Neighbourhood

"Where'd ya come from?"

That was the second question. Everyone who moves into a new development experiences being in at the birth of a neighbourhood. Wherever we came *from*, we were the ones who would create the unwritten traditions of this place. Into these, newcomers would be initiated, or from which, if they turned out to be dinkweeds, ostracized. We were lucky. A lot of big cedars and firs were left standing to cool and refresh the air on hot summer days. Cheap rock-gardens of tough perennials were our parents answer to the expansive arid front lawns trimmed with disposable annuals that uniformed the established neighbourhood of Forest Hills further down the mountain. But despite having moved to the edge of the wild, our parents couldn't help bringing that suburban 1950s "keeping up with the Jones's" luggage with them. Mothers agonized over whether to spend mornings or afternoons around a tubular chrome formica-topped kitchen table, without offending the women from the competing *kaffeeklatch* on the street. Fathers had to decide which husbands to trust with loaned tools or who to spend a precious day off with, helping finish his basement rumpus room in exchange for future considerations. As couples, they had to decide if they wanted to join the smart set whose social lives revolved around curling and drinking at the new fashionable 'winter clubs'—Canada's answer to the southern country club. Would they play bridge as a couple? Or would the husband requisition the knotty-pine panelled rumpus room for an all-male poker game once a week? These choices weren't trivial. They marked you socially as aspirant white-collar or recidivist blue.

Kids faced choices too. Would we call it Cowboys and Indians when we hunted each other through the woods, or Army, or simply Guns? Would we play ball hockey, baseball or touch football on the short flat section of our street? Would we be a Hide and Seek neighbourhood, or would Kick the Can be the dominant mode? Our choices would determine which games were passed on to younger brothers and sisters who'd pass them on in turn, an oral legacy, to new generations of neighbourhood kids. Our local dialect of schoolyard slang would evolve over the years, like a regional accent, into a code by which kids recognized each other and parents were kept universally ignorant of secret mischiefs.

## Exiles from Main Street

"The crimes were committed in the neighbourhood of Commercial and Broadway..."

Despite the neighbour part of the word, it's often misappropriated as an equivalent of vicinity, a geographical misconception that has become a truism of sloppy journalism and our intellectually lazy culture at large. This kind of false usage is insidious. Instead of factually reporting anti-social behaviour occurring within a geographically demarcated area of the city, it imputes criminal inclinations to *inhabitants* of that area in general. Gangsters, not usually noted for their mastery of the language, call it 'the hood' with rare accuracy, not to mention a nice play on words.

In West Vancouver in the 1960s, all teenage boys from North Vancouver were presumed to be "hoods." unworthy of the affections of daughters educated at downtown private schools like York House and Crofton House—girls whose virtue, by reputation at least, was an item of parental barter as the recently affluent sought to marry into bigger or older money. Those social-climbing West Van parents were wise to be leery of us. Nothing was as satisfying to a roaring North Van boy as fucking a spoiled West Van debutante speechless on a luxuriously sheeted parental bed, savouring the thrill of double violation, then having to dive out the window, leg it around the pool lights and into the shrubbery when the Caddy or Mercedes unexpectedly pulled into the garage.

Hitch-hiking home, more hiking than hitching, with tenderized testicles on a hot summer night, the dreamy perfume of broom and roses as intoxicating as the tidal fragrance lingering on your fingers, the memory of smooth cool thighs and belly tensed in nervous eagerness, still almost palpable, was so intense you wanted to peel off your drainpipe jeans and walk home bare-assed in the warm breeze. Back on your own turf, lying on your back in a little triangular sward of grass at Capilano Road and Edgemont with a long hill-climb ahead, you knew at seventeen life couldn't get any better than this. Snobbism isn't arbitrary. It always has some foundation in fact. Sociologists would have described our patchwork of blue and white collars as "middle class," though more than half the families were like ours. My father was a Vancouver fire fighter and my mother a housewife. They paid around $30,000 for the lot and house. As kids, we were turned loose on the edge of a wilderness, with raw forest for a park and half-built houses for gym equipment. To the dismay of our parents, who were working, scrimping and mortgaging their lives to provide a better environment for their kids—we went feral faster than escaped ferrets.

Every neighbourhood has a secret geography, an invisible map, like an overlay superimposed on the official grid; a hidden web of alleys, vacant lots, darkly shaded backyards with permeable fences, unlocked sheds and garages, sunken stairwells, all known to locals but as flat and innocuous as a theatre scrim in the glare of a police spotlight. In cities, some neighbourhoods become cities-within-cities where no watchman or constable dares enter except in force. Medieval Paris had the Court of Miracles, jointly ruled by the King of Beggars and the King of Thieves, London the notorious rookeries known as The Holy Land around New Oxford Street, Algiers its famous Casbah, sanctuary of villains like Pepe le Moko. New York has the South Bronx; Los Angeles, Watts and the *barrios*. Every American city has its inner city zone where the cops stay in cars, sweating in body armour, because they know what's good for them. Vancouver has the Block, the 100 block of Hastings east of Main, one of the meanest tenths of a mile in North America, immortalized by poet Bud Osborn, the Francois Villon of the East End, on his *Hundred Block Rock* CD, and by writer Joe Ferone in his brilliant tragic novel, *Boomboom*.

## Where Alph the Sacred River Ran

"...and stay away from the *creek*!"

Our mothers ended every daily pre-exodus lecture with that warning and every day we said, "Yes, Mom," lying through our demand-loan orthodontics. When we moved in, Mosquito Creek was a small but still wild river. Heavily wooded, it descended from Heaven like the Mother Ganga. A dunghill in Himalayan terms, Grouse Mountain barely tickles clouds I later got lost in more than once while hiking. Mist and rain the clouds offload trickles down countless seasonal streams into permanent creeks. Flanked by thick cedars and firs, Mosquito Creek runs through the heart of North Vancouver like an aorta, all the way down to the salt-chuck of Burrard Inlet.

Huge boulders, eight to ten feet across, formed natural dams restraining terraced pools of crystal water of equal depth. Shaded by drooping boughs, these were the swimming holes of nymphs, dryads and oriads, drinking fountains of the gods, and home to trout of twelve to twenty inches. Recognizing them as elemental, sacred places, we spent all our unsupervised time exploring the channels and small islands gathered around cedar roots that divided them. My brother Phil was born with the gift of being able to look at water without getting bored. This is the soul of angling. He used to sneak off to the creek with his little rod, a soup can of worms and fish a certain deep pool in which the Grand-Daddy Trout lurked, a 20-incher who must've weighed in at a couple of pounds.

A true angler knows patience is his most formidable weapon against the wily trout. Inevitably, Phil's paid off. He hooked the Grandad, played him and landed him fair and square. As the rush of triumph subsided, he realised if he took the fish home, Mom would know he'd been alone at the creek and tan his hide with the wooden spoon. A kindly neighbour was watching and offered to solve his dilemma by taking the incriminating trophy off his hands. He was what my Dad would have called "a real bastard," an epithet that has sadly lost most of its force due to social evolution.

## The Promised Land

"We're wreckin' the Skyliners' fort tomorrow! Pass it on."

We didn't inherit our section of the creek. Kids from a neighbourhood already built beyond the far bank had staked a claim to the mile or so of creek bed separating us. The Skyline Drive boys were about as happy to see us as the Canaanites and Moabites must've been when Joshua and the Hebrews showed up after forty years of chewing their sandals in the desert and announced that God had given *them* title to the real estate thereabouts.

Initial explorations of our wild playground went unchallenged. But when we started building tree-forts, just platforms at first, knocked up out of two-by-fours, shiplap and plywood lifted from the many active building sites in our area, we learned we'd have to fight for our right of occupation. We did it with the same mix of devious politics, sabotage, and passages of arms that adults were employing in the Cold War, then at its hottest.

Every time we returned to our forts we found them wrecked. We rebuilt, only to be wrecked again and again. As we explored the creek for signs of the miscreants, we were ambushed by volleys of missiles from alder and fir shadows on the far bank. We couldn't catch our attackers. Having been there longer, they knew the paths and game trails better than we did, especially on "their" side of the creek. Negotiations were attempted by heralds perched on rocks in the open creek-bed, calling out truce terms. "Stop wrecking our forts and we won't wreck yours!"

Glimpses of snickering boys in the undergrowth, shadows with cocked throwing arms.

"Fuck off, dinkweeds! You can't even *find* our fort! Stay out of the creek or we'll burn your fort down with you in it!"

Our emissaries fled under hard rains of punk, the approved ammunition for kid skirmishing. Small irregular blocks of wet rotted red cedar mined from old stumps, punk stung like a mad wasp when it connected with skin, but had the virtue of not being rock, which would've got us all involved with the adult world, so we could aim for each other's heads. A slab of punk in the eye, spreading stinging cedar shreds in the socket, was enough to render anybody *hors de combat*, screaming like a girl, never mind having to lie to your mother about how it got there.

Intelligence painstakingly gathered at Little League practice and Cub Scout meetings identified our adversaries, who went to Canyon Heights Elementary down in the Highlands, while we attended North Star, then Braemar, over toward Lonsdale. The school boundary, naturally, was the creek. Their ringleader was said to have the best fort on the whole creek, a pleasure-dome that not only boasted cedar-shake walls and roof, but actually had glass windows and electric light his father installed by rigging extension cords from their house through the trees.

Many an afternoon was spent on covert recon missions behind enemy lines, stealthy crawling through blackberry briars and bracken, until we found it, a quadrangular aerie suspended in four huge cedars. At the first opportunity, a public holiday when he and his gang would be away at family functions, we came down like "the wolf upon the fold" as the Bible says, except that we were armed with hammers, chisels and crowbars, the most fearsome weapons we could swipe from our fathers' toolboxes.

It was so obviously the incarnation of all kids' dreams of the Ideal Fort that we hesitated for a moment, as the Goths must once have paused at the gates of the fabled city of Rome. Then, like Greeks erupting from the wrong end of the Trojan Horse, we threw ourselves into a gang-rape of destruction while trying to keep the noise down—prying, ripping, tearing, gouging, smashing. Shakes and panes of glass were spun into the bush, studs torn loose and kicked away, the power line cut with a wild swing of a hatchet. When there was nothing left but the floor, we tore that up and cranked the joists loose until they fell into the weeds. Last one down the carefully-crafted ladder system demolished it with an axe as he descended. Possessed by berserker fury, we pissed and shat all over the debris before running for the creek, howling demented laughter.

Later we heard the boy whose fort it was cried when he saw what we'd done. I'd almost felt like crying myself as we danced up the rocks to our own rebuilt fort, a scrap-pile compared to the one we'd wrecked, yet I'd whooped and hooted as wildly as any Greek dancing among the toppled towers of Troy. Rumours circulated. His father was going to track us down and bring the cops to our houses, so we stayed close to home, suspiciously well-behaved for a week or so. At school, Cubs and baseball practice, we officially denied involvement in what was, in its time, as famous a fort-wrecking as the Sack of Rome.

The angry father never appeared at our doors. The great Skyline fort was never rebuilt. Our denials were officially accepted, privately doubted. At school and in surrounding neighbourhoods we acquired a reputation for Viking ferocity. More than a week after going to ground, we returned to the creek to find our pathetic fort miraculously intact. None of the half dozen gangs who had forts in the creek had dared touch it, not even to write swear words on the walls in stolen school chalk. We'd won our turf.

## Exodus

"Run for the creek!"

Overhung by big trees, Mosquito Creek was a nearly subterranean passageway into other worlds. Within it, we were invisible, untouchable, like Norsemen rowing shallow-draft dragon ships up an unsuspecting English estuary. Emerging out of the ravine, we could appear suddenly in any neighbourhood bordering the creek to steal bikes carelessly left lying at the ends of driveways, maybe even B&E an empty house that backed on the ravine, making off with jars of coins, a package of frozen wieners, bottles of warm beer from a case in the basement, half a pack of cigarettes left on a kitchen counter.

Mostly we just swaggered through unfamiliar streets looking tough until some scared little kid told his big brother, who called his friends, or a neighbour didn't recognize us or like our looks and called the cops. Then we'd run, always instinctively making for the sanctuary of the creek. Big granite boulders were strewn down its bed like a Giant's Causeway. If you had good sneakers and good nerves, knew to dodge the ones tinged green with slippery moss and were absolutely fearless in your trust of gravity, momentum and perfect reflexes, you could actually *run* the rocks in a linked sequence of flying leaps executed flat-out with grace and precision that would have most Olympic hurdlers knocking back Valium just thinking about it.

Often we'd run the rocks for fun, two or three miles down to the bridge at Queens Road, stroll into the small Edgemont shopping centre, fill our pockets with penny candy swiped from the Totem Five & Dime or Casper's Drugs, slouch around the corner to the bus stop and catch a Highlands bus that would drop us off a hundred yards from where we started our run. On slow summer afternoons, we'd do it twice.

I can't explain *how* we performed feats that would defy the reflexes and credulity of Olympic champions. I only recall the feeling of pure empty perfection that lingers somewhere deep in my synaptic and muscle memory. I rediscover it in emergencies when I shift my weight an inch, as if I already *know* what will happen next in the micro-sequence of events that incrementally make up an accident, enabling me to transform the event, like a linebacker making an interception because he's *read* the play subconsciously from visual cues and knows where the ball will be before it's even thrown.

Store keepers and cops also know how to read body language and team play. They recognized us, not their own local troublemakers, but as Visigoths and Vandals from the Hyrcanian Forest up the creek. One day as we scuffed up dust across Highlands Elementary schoolyard, our pockets bulging with swiped Smarties, purloined Pixy Stix, scoffed jawbreakers and hooked Snickers bars, two RCMP cruisers tried to take us in a pincer movement.

Bolting like weasels from a charnel henhouse, we shredded our Keds running for the creek a long block away. A stride ahead of the converging cars and thumping cop boots, we bailed blind, like paratroopers on a night drop, into thick blackberry briars that fenced the banks more effectively than barbed wire. We knew there was just enough space under the thickets for slim feral boys to slide through with faith and minimal blood loss. While the Mounties flailed and cursed and got their uniforms stained with blood and blackberry juice, we were running up the rocks like jackrabbit acrobats, laughing like loons. We were still laughing as we danced up the rocks around a bend in the creek, halfway home, and saw two more Mounties patrolling one of the yellow-painted wooden bridges that crossed it at several points.

Dodging into flanking forest trails we knew by heart, we backtracked around the bend, separated into pairs and threes, and exited the ravine on opposite sides onto crescent streets off Highlands Road and Delbrook Avenue. From there, we hopped buses that dropped us off half a block from the yellow bridge on Montroyal Avenue, where yet *another* Mountie was still waiting for us to appear.

He gave us the hard eye, but we sauntered into our neighbourhood whistling like we were on our way home from Bible study. Ducking into a half-framed house, we divided our loot and gorged like hogs, hunkered down behind concrete and plywood while the cops cruised the neighbourhood for hours. We watched cop cars roaring around and red-faced Mounties stomping up and down waving flashlights as it got dark and close to dinner time. Silently, invisibly, we bugged-out down hidden trails, vaulted or slipped under neighbour's fences and innocently sat down to dinner. When our mothers asked what we'd been up to all afternoon as they dished up the macaroni and cheese or tuna casserole, we all gave the same answer.

"Nothin' much."

## Heart of Darkness

"We called and called," our mothers said, "Where *were* you?"

"Just *around*," we all lied.

The creek also ran in the other direction, deeper into the wilderness, up into the clouds. Cautiously, groups of boys and girls investigated like the first European explorers who sought the headwaters of great rivers. In addition to being our Mother Ganga, our Thames, our Seine, main artery of our micro-civilisation, Mosquito Creek was our Nile, our Amazon, our Congo or Zambezi—our River of Mystery, gateway into the Great Unknown.

The uppermost of the yellow painted road bridges crossed the creek only a block north of our fort. Stinking of creosote, its under-structure of heavy beams was adorned with long quotations from the Bible, executed in neat block letters with white paint. Some big rocks in the creek bore the same writing in red. You'd find them by accident, running the rocks or exploring a new pool, usually short exhortations like JESUS SAVES; more often the one word admonition: REPENT.

It was spooky, especially above the bridge where the channel narrowed and the banks got steeper, to know they could only be meant for the eyes of the rare lost soul who would actually follow the slippery ankle-breaking creek bed into the unknown, someone like you. Once we got used to them, cheekier boys would add tags turning one into JESUS SAVES BEER BOTTLES. Later generations favoured JESUS SAVES AND RICHARD SCORES ON THE

REBOUND. None of us ever REPENTed, until much later, when it was too late.

As we climbed, alders closed in overhead, creating a permanent greenish twilight. Slime thickened on rocks like mould on a tuna sandwich left in a school locker. Dark and thus bottomless, pools vibrated with water-skippers and the creek lived up to its name. Stifling air rang with the whine of blood-sucking bugs. We crawled and stumbled and slapped ourselves through the murk like Wingate's Chindits in the Burmese jungle.

Skeeters, heat, wet, exhaustion, the approach of dinnertime, superstitious fear of the dark, imagined bears, cougars, maybe even wolves, watching and waiting, or something else—the Nameless Dread from childhood that all great explorers have felt on journeys into the country of the unknown—something always drove us back from the ultimate prize. Retreating to the sanctuary of our scrap-built fort, we'd draw crude maps and rehash our adventures like members of the Explorers Club settling into wingback chairs and getting into the vintage port.

We knew the source must be *there*, just beyond the edge of the map, just around the next bend in the creek. If only we hadn't started so late. If only we'd realized the creek would get shallow and stagnant and we'd need canteens of fresh water. If only we'd brought some candy bars. If only I hadn't twisted my ankle slipping on that slick rock.

We never told our parents or other kids where we were going or when we'd be back. No one knew where we were. That was part of the adventure. Myths, legends and true stories of real life heroism had taught us explorers achieved greatness when they went beyond hope of rescue, like Leif Erickson or Columbus crossing the Atlantic, Scott and Shackleton in the Antarctic, Burton and

Speke seeking the source of the Nile, Burke and Wills looking for Australia's phantom inland sea and Franklin's doomed search for the Northwest Passage.

Later, we read Golding's *Lord of the Flies* and Conrad's *Heart of Darkness* as junior high school English assignments. We recognized the experience of Piggy and the boys and Marlowe and Kurtz as something we'd already found—awe and terror, fear and trembling at the edge of the savage world—right in our own neighbourhood.

## The Great Flood

"The creek's over the bank! The yellow bridge is gone!"

Floods caused by a Pacific cyclone in 1962 resulted in the creek channel being dynamited and bulldozed into an innocuous ditch to protect the incipient upper middle class from having their real estate values literally eroded. Overnight, it became ugly and dull, the mid-channel islands of firs and cedars that sheltered our forts gone as if they'd been hit with a tactical nuclear bomb. The bulldozers cut more than a flood channel—they cut the heart out of the neighbourhood.

That wild heart used to beat a different rhythm every season. A sound you hardly heard, like white noise, you became aware of it only when you got too far away to hear it. You heard it in your sleep, waking in winter and spring storms to the rumble of boulders bowled by the force of the creek, softer but scarier than thunder. The creek was the hidden pulse of the neighbourhood. With it silenced, we became part of the vast tame suburbs of Vancouver's North Shore.

Suburbs embody our secular culture's stylized concept of Paradise. Blue skies and white clouds bless manicured greenswards attended not by invisible angelic florists and groundskeepers but by their earthly counterparts, mostly itinerant hippies who have replaced the ubiquitous Japanese gardeners of the Sixties. The mountain-climbing suburbs of North and West Vancouver are a landscape gardener's Stairway to Heaven, which is why the "best" people build mansions at the retreating tree-line, where the view induces vertigo, the altitude a nose-bleed and the price of property a panic attack. That these houses are well above the snow line, sometimes impossible to reach by car in bad winters, detracts from their absurdly inflated value not one obsolete red cent.

Though some old trees remain, they're oddly stunted. In a kind of Suburban Bonsai, for decades residents have paid handsomely to have their lower neighbours' trees topped to maximize their own view of the increasingly ugly Vancouver skyline. Rockeries have been replaced, their natural contours sculpted into level terraces by new owners who can afford trucked-in fill, topsoil, pre-grown lawn that comes rolled up like carpet on a flatbed, and professional landscapers who trim it weekly and charge ten times what the neighbour boy did back in the 1960s.

So much well-tended grass with nobody playing on it. Suburbs are now built with the marketing lure of actually being *part of* a golf course, the quintessential expression of man's taming of the wilderness and the bourgeois idea of what Heaven will look like. Even as a paperboy fifty years ago, I sensed the eerie aesthetic congruity of the suburb, the golf course and the cemetery.

## Paradise Sold

*"Location! Location! Location!"*
—Real estate mantra.

Fuelled by Baby Boomers settling down to raise families, the real estate boom of the 1980s wrote a premature epitaph for our neighbourhood. I'd drive up to our old house, turn off the car and listen. Instead of the chorus of falsetto shrieks our mothers once used to track our location, I heard nothing but silence and distant sirens. I didn't have to drive around lacrosse or hockey sticks, baseball bats, bicycles, skateboards and the wrecked soapbox racers that littered the streets when I was a kid.

The abrupt escalation of property values snapped the saliva thread of oral transmission by which the bedrock values of a real neighbourhood are conveyed. By the mid-1980s, working class families could no longer afford to live where I grew up. Those who could were the kind of dual-income professional partnerships that surrender their children to nannies at birth, then to private schools and extracurricular regimes that take them out of the neighbourhood; couples whose demanding careers let them spend very little time in their extensively renovated designer-decorated homes, yet who bitch that they don't know their neighbours as an indictment of contemporary society over *crème brûlée* in some downtown bistro.

My mother sold our house too early in the boom to garner the huge windfall profits some would reap when Asian businessmen, nervous about the looming return of Hong Kong to China, got into cell phone bidding wars for houses they hadn't even seen, seeking safe havens for their families and their money. My mother sold because she was lonely in that big house, surrounded by all those multi-bedroom boxes tenanted by aging couples, old birds in emptied nests, all wishing they lived in apartments or townhouses without big yards and gardens to maintain, closer to the mall and the doctor's office, but hanging on to max out their equity so their grown children would have serious money to fight over when they died.

A year or two before my mother sold, I moved to a studio apartment over a garage on Bewicke Avenue. It backed onto lower Mosquito Creek, barely three blocks north of where it voids discreetly into Burrard Inlet. I walked my dog, Nell, along its rough paths—since improved by municipal minions into an overdesigned *trail system*, complete with dog-poop bag dispensers; the New World Order notion of recreational green space. Most Sundays, I'd drive up to our old house for my one square meal of the week, but one Sunday it occurred to me that Nell and I could walk up to William Griffin Park on Queens, as we usually did, and just keep going up the creek. We'd come out less than a block from my mother's house, just like we used to do as kids.

It was good use of a sunny afternoon. The '63 cyclone had swamped the Queens Road bridge under three feet of brown mud. In retaliation city planners buried the ford and a mile long section of the creek above it in a square concrete tunnel. But above this huge culvert, as Nell and I loafed along, I could see the creek slowly trying, with each spring runoff, to rearrange itself in a natural pattern, sculpting and shifting boulders an inch per season, excavating pools, trying to recover its memory of itself.

Along the banks, fragmented sections of our old trails had escaped the dozer blades. I stumbled through them, led by Nell's nasal instinct for exploration. It was like trying to follow pieces of a shredded map. The creek was a ghost of itself. Walking it that afternoon haunts me more than the moment my brother Phil and I moved the last of my mother's things out of our old house and sat on the empty living room floor trying to feel something about a neighbourhood that no longer existed except in our memories.

## Because It's There

While living on Bewicke, I re-connected with Karel Groeneveld, a high school friend. A new guide to the trails of the North Shore had just been published. We decided to climb every peak on the North Shore skyline. We had dogs to walk and it beat mowing lawns, cleaning out the garage or anything else his wife or my girlfriends would've had us do, with one possible exception.

When we talked about what we were doing with friends, we noticed how few people who live and work in Vancouver and look at that skyline every day, even people who grew up on a slant on the North Shore, ever bother to climb to the height of land and look at what's on the other side. Lots of people take the Skyride up Grouse Mountain, but from the Chalet the view is *back*, toward Vancouver and the thickening belt of smog over Surrey we watched turn from yellow to brown in a couple of short summers as the suburbs pushed deeper into the Fraser Valley.

To see the other side, you have to hike about an hour beyond the Chalet on easy trails to the peak of Goat Mountain, or push on to Crown Mountain if you're frisky. More Vancouverites do this now than in the past, but it's still a small club. As adults, most of us know our own city in the same way we knew our neighbourhoods as kids, recognizing boundaries between the familiar and unfamiliar which, out of habit, become barriers to imagination as well.

When we think, most of us think about things we already know, or at least know something about. This passes for common sense among our species. If you don't *know* about something, how can you *think* about it? Lucky for us, some members of our mob grow up to be scientists and philosophers who spend most of their lives thinking about what they *don't* know. If they didn't, we'd have been extinct before we invented the pointed stick.

What's on the other side of the first rampart of Coast Mountains is more mountains, sheathed in fir and cedar, as far as the mind can see. No subdivisions, no houses, no roads except a few logging tracks and very few rough trails. Step out onto that north-east slope, it's hundreds of miles of unforgiving wilderness to the next Tim Hortons. You're looking at the Edge of the World as you know it, standing on a line that old maps would have indicated with a warning legend, "Beyonde heere are monsteres."

"There is no wilderness in Europe," my friend Ed Fischer told me when he returned from a trip to Austria and Germany tracking his own roots. "You can hike for hours, come around the last turn in the trail and at the summit there's a gasthaus with hot schnitzel, cold beer and a band playing polka music, all hauled up by a service gondola. Even if there isn't, as soon as you reach the height of land anywhere in Europe and start hiking down into the next valley, you come to farms and hamlets. You're hiking back *in* to civilisation, not *out*."

Ed and I had hiked together erratically since our teens. We'd climb the Lions every so often and bushwhack the North Shore woods on tracks that have since been improved and incorporated into the Baden-Powell Trail and other "systems" now favoured by mobs of spandex commandos every weekend. Back in the Sixties, the only people we ever met in the bush wore leather shorts and spoke with East European or German accents. Now he knew why.

"The reason all we met were immigrants on the trails years ago was that they came from places where wilderness no longer exists except as a mythic culture-memory of the ancient Hyrcanian Forest. They were in awe because here, there's really nothing out there for hundreds of miles but wilderness." That awe is a deep primal connection to the past. You don't have to hike for hundreds of miles unless you're a masochistic purist. All you need do is take one small step across the habitual boundary of your imagination and you're back at the moment the chimp fell out of the tree and instead of climbing back up to the safety of the known world of the forest canopy, stood up...and walked out onto an alien savannah.

## A Creek Runs Through It

"Ascent from here is neither difficult nor attractive."
—Bruce Fairley, *A Guide to Climbing & Hiking in Southwestern British Columbia*; Entry for Fromme Mountain.

While Ed was trekking in India and Nepal, chasing the phantom snow leopard and the meaning of life, Karel and I pursued our more modest mountaineering project in a less reverent spirit. We applied Post-modern radical juxtaposition theory to counter the onslaught of granola-crunching pseudo-purists, duded up in Gore-Tex fetish-wear, who were beginning to crowd the trails. I dressed in Full Hemingway Drag; plaid shirts and a battered old fedora with trout flies in the band, baggy military surplus fatigue pants with big cargo pockets and surplus Italian Army mountain troop boots.

We despised the lame shit trendy hikers ate. *No Trail Mix* was our rule. Especially no *Gorp*, the one-pot muck regarded as the *Chateaubriand* of alpine cuisine. Instead, we discovered Tupperware and pre-packaged gourmet foods like canned Danish Camembert and Brie cheeses, which soften to ideal consistency in a rucksack during a four hour hike. We packed dry salami, cold chicken, olives, hummus and Greek salads in airtight containers. We carried sixers of beer and litres of wine instead of water. Anyone who can't find the best drinking water in the world running off the North Shore mountains should stay in the bar and order another Perrier. On a cool fall day-hike up Strachan Mountain, Karel horrified a bunch of nut-crunchers on the summit when he pulled out a big Thermos of espresso, lined up a rack of airline liqueur miniatures on a rock and invited orders for exotic coffees.

It was on one of these irreverent hikes I finally found the elusive Grail of my youth, the source of the stream of water that seems to run like a major artery through so many neighbourhoods I've lived in, harping to be turned into some kind of symbol or metaphor. From childhood, I spent some of the best days of my life along Mosquito Creek. I fished it, swam in it, saw my first girl naked beside it when we dared each other to take off our bathing suits in a hidden clearing in the woods near our old tree fort. Years later, I made furtive ecstatic love with women I especially adored in secret places discovered while walking my dog along the lower creek twice a day.

Walking Nell, I used to stop and sit, cross-legged and shirtless, on one of the few surviving big boulders, an island in the stream where the sun cut through the overhanging cedars like a blade of light. The cool breeze, the soft wet whisper of water and the warmth of the sun seemed to fill my body to a joyous bursting, a state of grace that left no room for thought...This isn't quite *A River Runs Through It*, I know, but I'm making the most of what I have.

## Water of life

Karel and I parked at the top of Prospect Road, walked the eager dogs down through the alders and there it was—a shadowed slippery quicksilver trickle between big un-bulldozed boulders—exactly as I remembered when it drove us back in frustration and secret fear four decades before. This was the Dread Limit of the World, pericardium of the Heart of Darkness. Now, my Subaru wagon was parked forty steps away.

We followed the stream using a tangle of old logging tracks along its flanks, letting the dogs run free to get high on the heady scents of coyote and bear piss. Eventually we reached the Cascade, a giant logjam of stumps, boulders and packed silt congealed into a geographic feature over which the creek falls. On that stifling August day, it barely stumbled. Above the Cascade, we lurched out of the bush onto the alder-flanked private gravel track that services Grouse Mountain from the top of Lynn Valley Road. There was no traffic other than that indicated by fresh bear scat.

Across the road, a single-file trail took us up Mount Fromme. To give Bruce Fairley his due, it wasn't "difficult," except for the heat and the bugs, nor was it "attractive," except for ripe wild blueberries staining our legs and filling our mouths and the quiet joy of being out in the woods instead of sitting in some air-conditioned fern bar grazing on overpriced appies and trying not to lose two hundred dollar sunglasses. Rills and streamlets from the east slope of Grouse, the southwest side of Thunderbird Ridge and the south slope of Fromme, all drain the rain into Mosquito Creek, but I'd been surprised to see on maps in Fairley's guidebook that the main line of the creek arced not up Grouse, as I'd always assumed it must, but to a small lake on the south peak of its less distinguished neighbour, Mount Fromme.

That day I hiked with no special sense of mission, just a kind of suppressed excitement masked by sweaty nonchalance. If one of the dogs had gone lame, if a thunderstorm had rained us off the heights, I wouldn't have been surprised or disappointed. Experience had pretty much convinced me I was destined never to see the headwaters of Mosquito Creek.

It was waiting for us at the top—a big pond suspended in a pocket of mossy rock below the summit—strafed by dragonflies, clogged with lily pads, riotous with frogs. Yet, with the rock escarpment of the north peak as a backdrop, it was as perfectly composed as a Japanese water garden. Sitting down in the damp sedge, we stared in silence while the grateful dogs slurped in the shallows.

"Fuck what the book says. This is worth the hike," Karel said.

He'd grown up in Lynn Valley, too far east of Mosquito Creek for it to have been part of his history, and our hike had been a dull sticky bushwhack. If he was impressed, I didn't need to say anything. I lifted a litre of red wine out of my knapsack and we saluted the little nameless lake, source of what has been the water of life to me for as long as I can remember. I hoisted one for the Creek kids, all the neighbour boys and girls sucked away by gravity and time, flowing like water toward Vancouver and other cities, other countries and continents, who never saw this simple thing, a pool of semi-stagnant water glittering and quivering with life like Eden's enchanted septic tank on a summer afternoon.

Because they never saw it, the men and women those boys and girls became may have forgotten the intensity of our failed first quests beyond the neighbourhood; how we overcame our fear of the unfamiliar and set out to be heroes, to plant our ragged homemade flag in a place we only imagined on scrawled foolscap maps. I wish I could show them that the secret heart of our old neighbourhood turned out to be something so beautiful, so simple. It endures; a microcosmic source of life pouring out in a stream, indifferent to the suburban wastelands of contrived cookie-cutter neighbourhoods it passes through in its downward course to what poet Peter Trower calls "the angelus ocean"—the great all-creating, all-devouring, planet-girdling sea that is the mother of the world. Having seen it at last, I know that I will never lose the sense of what it felt like to be a child, ignorant but insatiably curious, determined to be brave, venturing out into the great and boundless world unknown.

FOUR

# Bad Haircuts

## Herman the German

When I was a kid every Vancouver neighbourhood seemed to have a barber we all hated and feared, a Teutonic headsman parents threatened to send you to if you kicked up about getting a haircut. "Well, if you're going to make a fuss, we'll just have to send you to Herman the German from now on. He gives a proper boy's haircut and he's cheaper besides." Even *they* called him Herman the German.

Our Herman was cheap because he worked out of a jerry-rigged tonsorial torture chamber in the front room of his run-down house. The house was as old and creepy as Herman himself. Blistered paint, spavined steps, a peaked shake roof almost completely devoured by moss, sad curtains. Nobody ever saw the woman he rarely referred to as *"mine vife."* Naturally, all the kids said she was a witch.

If you were sent to Herman's, you begged or bribed your best friend with your most precious baseball cards to come with you. Terrible stories circulated about nameless kids who had gone to Herman's alone. Whispered tales of hideous mutilations and no-kidding outright disappearances whipped around the schoolyard backstops like a winter wind.

Inside, the only bright spots in the dingy front room were an ancient stove-iron pedestal chair with cracked enamel armrests and a fraying stained leather seat, and the steel tray in which Herman kept his 'instruments.' The linoleum floor had been yellow maybe back in the 1930s. Around the chair, the floor was spotted with dark stains, rumoured to be the blood of Herman's victims. One battered chrome and vinyl kitchen chair occupied a corner.

"You are vanting a haircut alzo?" Herman would demand of an accomplice who dared to sit on it. *"Neh? Vell, ziz chair iz fur pipple who are vaiting fur ein haircut! You vill stillgestand und vait, if not!"*

Nobody ever sat in that chair. Nobody was ever waiting for a haircut at Herman the German's. There was no table beside the chair and nothing to read, no old copies of *Field and Stream* or *Argosy*, or *True Detective* magazine, whose covers featured bound, blonde women, their clothes ripped to expose exciting curves of breast and thigh, eyes and mouths gaping as the huge shadows of homicidal maniacs loomed over them. I doubt Herman even knew what a comic book was.

We did. Comics like *Sgt. Rock*, *Weird War Tales* and *True War Stories*. Their plots borrowed a lot from Rod Serling's popular *Twilight Zone* TV series, frequently involving haunted tanks manned by zombie Nazis who wouldn't die and ghosts of soldiers from bygone wars materializing to fight on the side of the heroes. The Nazis were always led by tall, sharp-jawed German officers who bragged of sadistic atrocities and whose arrogance was their undoing when the good guys charged into their midst, combat knives clenched in grimacing jaws, tommy guns fire-spitting *Brrattatatat!* and *Budda-Budda-Budda-Bam!* To us, the Nazi officers all looked like Herman the German. We didn't dare bring our own comics with us when we got a haircut.

Regular barbershops kept stacks of magazines like *True* and *Male* handy. Wads of cheap newsprint in glossy covers, between the grainy black and white glamour photos of young women in risqué two-piece bathing suits, they featured stories about hunters battling man-eating grizzlies and sport fishing for sharks. One of their staple features in the 1950s was the sensational news that some famous Nazi or other was living in luxury in a Central or South American country, heavily guarded by former SS stormtroopers and man-eating Dobermans. For some reason Hitler's chief boot-licker, Martin Bormann, was the subject of most of these articles. We weren't too clear on what Bormann had done, but the theory propounded by the articles—that former Nazi bigshots were alive and living pretty well, having escaped justice at the Nuremburg Trials—seemed to undermine our suspicions that Herman the German was a war criminal in hiding. I voiced my misgivings to my friend Paul as we pored over fuzzy photos of Bormann's supposed villa in the jungles of Paraguay.

"But, Herman the German doesn't have any SS guards or killer dogs. If he really is some Nazi with a hoard of stolen gold, why isn't he living like that? Why is he cutting hair and living in a dumpy house that smells like nobody ever takes the garbage out?"

Nothing could stifle Paul's *Hardy Boys* enthusiasm.

"That's just it! He's smarter than Bormann and those other Nazis! The reporters found them. They haven't found Herman because he's fiendishly clever. By pretending to be just a cheap barber and hiding out here instead of in South America, he's probably the cleverest and evilest Nazi of all."

Fiendish cleverness was understood to be an essential skill for arch-criminals in general, but I always wondered how the Nazis cultivated this rather specialized talent. At school, we'd been given intelligence quotient and aptitude tests whose results were forwarded to school boards and government statisticians. Had the Nazi Party made Germans take some kind of similar test, specially rigged to reveal fiendish cleverness?

It was hard to argue with Paul. He had discovered the pornography of historical violence, more intoxicating than the *Playboy* magazines our fathers hid in closets or under beds, right there in the family living room in his Dad's collection of books about the war. Many of the cheap paperbacks claimed to be actual memoirs of German U-boat Captains, SS officers and camp commandants. But while Paul quoted them to breathless boys in after-school basements, I had reservations about the latter. After all, would anyone guilty of torturing and murdering thousands, if not millions of people, a man wanted for crimes against humanity, write a book about it and collect his royalties? Maybe. It just didn't seem likely.

I kept my misgivings to myself. Paul had all those books to back him up and the rapt attention of the other boys, all committed to unmasking Herman the German as the war criminal, former saboteur, or Gestapo agent we convinced ourselves he was. It was only a matter of time and sly counter-espionage before we would take our case to the Mounties, get medals from all the Allied governments and get our pictures in the paper. When our parents sent us to Herman the German for haircuts, we accepted our fate the way a spy accepts a dangerous mission. Herman the German always gave us something to report at rumpus-room debriefings over Cokes and barbecue potato chips.

## Evidence

Evidence: Herman was a lousy barber. Aha! Obviously not his original trade, but one learned hurriedly for his fake cover identity.

Evidence: No matter what kind of haircut you asked for, Herman gave you the lice-defying pig-shave common to both SS men and concentration camp inmates. Aha!

Evidence: Herman always drew blood. Aha! A monster who'd waded in human blood must be addicted to the sight of it, like Bela Lugosi in *Dracula*. His dull clippers always seemed to snag the tender cartilage of an ear, bringing out the notorious stinging styptic pencil, followed by sullen yowlings and incomprehensible oaths. It was always our own fault, "fur sqvirmink zo much!"

Evidence: Herman had a tattoo. I was the one who discovered it. Feeling the shears catch an earlobe, I bucked forward away from the blades. A bony claw snapped me back into the iron embrace of the chair. Emerging from the frayed white cuff speckled with brown bloodstains, a thin wrist, a forearm displaying a sequence of faded blue numbers distorted by age and liver spots.

Aha.

Paul had come with me in exchange for overnight use of my new unread *Mad* magazine and to spy on Herman. When we were back on the street, my head rapidly chilling under residual peach fuzz, I passed on my information.

"Herman was in the camps."

Paul smacked his fist into his other palm.

"I knew it! I wonder how many Jews he killed?" He began to sing a parody of the Pillsbury cookie dough TV commercial jingle: *"Nothin' says lovin' like shovin' them in the oven..."*

"No, dink-weed. I mean he was in the camps. He has the tattoo."

Paul was thrilled.

"That must be his SS blood group tattoo!"

"That's on the inside of the upper arm, remember? You read it from that book. Herman's tattoo is too far down, just above his wrist."

Paul lowered his voice to a conspirator's whisper, his eyes on fire.

"It must be a Wehrmacht serial number. Y'know the Russians ordered the execution of captured Germans with a tattoo on their arms because they found out about the SS blood group tattoo. They even executed regular German soldiers from certain regiments who had tattoos..."

I couldn't listen to any more of it.

"Paul, Herman isn't a war criminal, or a spy or a Nazi hiding out with a suitcase full of gold teeth he knocked out of the mouths of dead Jews. He was a prisoner in the camps. He didn't kill any Jews. He probably is a Jew."

The mythologies of male adolescence are precious camouflage, counterfeit of the impossible certainties of manhood. Knowing everything about war, sex, cars and sports substitutes for not having done or being able to do anything. You have to be able to say, *Yeah, sure, what else is new?* about everything.

If you stand in wide-eyed wonder and admit you don't know what a hat-trick is, who won the war and how, the uses of slicks and radials, that women sometimes bleed *down there*, you're a goof or worse, you're back in kindergarten, your world shattered by somebody's revelation that Santa Claus, the Easter Bunny and the Tooth Fairy are really just your parents.

"Mom? Can I have my Masturbation Papers?"

She looks like she's been slapped, then she starts to laugh, her hand over her mouth. Even in the immediate conciliatory hug, you can still feel her laughing, silently, and she's laughing at you, not with you. Arteries at least wait for old age to become sclerotic. Invisibly scarring the heart, attitudes harden at puberty.

"No! It's his SS tattoo! He's a fucking Nazi! Herman the German! Herman the German!"

Paul was shouting like a monk exhorting a brother, flirting with heresy by bellowing the rosary to shout down blasphemy. He wasn't going to believe me. He couldn't. If Herman the German wasn't really a Nazi war criminal or a spy, what other essential truths discovered in our basement symposiums might prove false? Uncertainty, anarchy, chaos implicit. Boys are perfect philosophers. I backed down.

"Well, maybe...I guess..."

I knew at that moment on the sidewalk outside Herman the German's decrepit house that somewhere inside, in the kind of tiny invisible space that hides a tumour, my friend Paul had begun to hate me, though he didn't know it yet.

## Double Agent

So I became a spy, a double agent, and the first thing I found out was the truth about what Paul's Dad did in the war. Every boy our age had asked his father, "What did you do in the war, Dad?" Most of our fathers who fought the Germans in Europe or the Japanese in the Pacific were tight-mouthed about their experiences. They did not keep books about the war around the house. Only Paul's must've been different because by Paul's account his Dad seemed to have battled both the Krauts and the Japs in every major theatre of the war.

I found out simply by asking my Dad. It was the kind of thing men in the neighbourhood knew about each other from talking over the fence, at barbecues and bridge parties. By the time Paul's father was old enough to enlist, the Germans had surrendered. He was still in training, bombarding the empty spaces of Saskatchewan with sacks of flour when the atomic bomb ended the war with Japan.

"He doesn't know how lucky he was," my Dad told me quietly.

Paul began avoiding me, taking most of our friends with him for reasons they didn't understand. To them, I was just being a sulky spoilsport who wanted to play baseball instead of kick-the-can.

One night months later, Herman the German's old house burned down in twenty minutes, incinerating Herman and his wife. One of the boys told me Paul was saying the fire was proof that Herman was a Nazi. The Israelis had recently kidnapped Adolf Eichmann from Argentina and were putting him on trial because he was such an important war criminal. It was too hard to kidnap someone out of Canada, Paul said, so Israeli agents had burned Herman's house down with him in it, the way he had burned the Jews. When this secret was confided in the boy's washroom at school, I laughed out loud within earshot of Paul, knowing he was watching my reaction. The fire marshal blamed old knob-and-tube wiring.

Paul's hate festered and fostered mine in time we measured in school grades until, four years later, we had it out in a fight, well-advertised on the junior high school jungle telegraph and staged in front of a crowd of hundreds in the parking lot of a strip mall where we now got bad haircuts from a foul-tempered Italian at Frank's Barbershop. Paul and I danced around for ten minutes, flicking the boots at each other without making contact until I taunted him.

"Guess you think Frank is Mussolini's kid brother, eh?"

Nobody else knew why he suddenly went crazy, charged and smacked me one on the nose that squirted blood all over Frank's window. Doing it brought him close enough for me to kick him in the nuts so hard he buckled over and fell down gasping like a bloated fish. Before I could give him the obligatory stomping, a huge RCMP constable and our school vice-principal—who'd actually lost part of a leg to a German land mine in the war—lofted us both into the back of a police car and drove us back to school. After a verbal reaming from both of them, we stumbled home together.

I couldn't stop touching my possibly broken nose. Paul walked bow-legged, trying not to jiggle his tender gonads. We talked about girls and cars and how stupid it was for us to fight because we'd been friends since we were kids. It was only because other kids at school loved to promote fights that we wound up in deep shit—with the cops, who now had our names in their little black notebooks, and with Mr. Mayo, who was going to keep us in detention until we graduated. Neither of us said a word about Herman the German.

## The Persistence of Memory

We never fought again, but we were never friends again either. The real reason got lost in time, a part of childhood as impossible to recapture as Christmas morning wonder. Memory is ephemeral. It has no leverage against history. History has a physical presence; it's in books. I never forgot Herman the German and I remembered Paul well enough to recognize him more than twenty years later, selling home insulation from behind a display table in a North Vancouver mall I'd stopped at because I needed a birthday gift for my wife and a bottle of wine for dinner at my sister's house. I don't like canned air, Muzak or crowds, so normally I'd have used the outside entrances to the stores. But it was raining, so I shuffled through the crowed mall. Not the first time weather has been the hand of fate and it won't be the last.

Paul had more hair on the backs of his hands than on his head. You could've shot hoops with his gut. He congratulated me for not having aged so badly. I lied and told him he looked great as we updated our resumes. I had survived divorce, clinical depression, alcoholism and the thousand ills the flesh of writers is heir to—to wind up happily married with three kids that were teaching me the meaning of life.

"I heard you got a book published, so I got it. I really liked the story..."

I modestly cut that subject short because one of the characters in my autobiographical first novel had been so obviously based on him he couldn't have missed it, if he'd really read it. It wasn't a flattering portrait, yet he didn't seem pissed.

"Glad you liked it. What've you been up to?"

He was happy to have the subject changed to himself. Most people are. It's the easiest way to keep the conversational canoe out of whitewater. He'd married a girl whose name I dimly recalled from our high school cheerleading roster, though I couldn't get a visual, but he clearly expected me to be impressed. They were divorced, but he assured me he took an active role in the co-parenting of their daughter. That took all of twenty seconds. Then he told me he'd made "a million-five" in some real estate deal, but his money was tied up because his partners had cut some corners, "nothing illegal, just technical stuff," which caused the SEC to get bitchy, so his assets were frozen while it was, "before the courts." Meanwhile, he was paying alimony and child support. "Not that I mind, but it would be nice if the courts cut a guy some slack when he's dashing from a civil action in one room down to family court in another." That part took longer.

"I'm just doing this to help out a friend in the insulation business." He gestured to the literature on the table casually, as if he'd noticed I wasn't showing visible symptoms of frostbite. "I threw some work his way when I was developing properties, but things are a bit slow just now, so he asked me to stand in while he supervises some jobs. One hand washes the other. It's not what you know but who you know. Contacts, networking, that's what makes it all happen..."

Commerce had replaced historically legitimized violence as Paul's rhetorical mode of choice. He'd become one of those guys whose small talk is of markets, mutual funds, stocks versus bonds, lending rates, property values, peppered with financial acronyms and references to 'my broker' and 'my accountant'—a guy whose confidences were always about vague 'deals' soon to generate fabulous wealth. In the way he had once believed in the Odessa, the supposed secret post-war SS organization, he now believed in the power of business cabals who prospered through the mysterious efficacy of 'networking.'

He began telling me about new projects 'coming on-stream.' I started to feel like I was being hustled. He was treating me like some best-selling author with more dollars than sense who might be looking for an investment opportunity to sink a huge publisher's advance into. I tried to tell him what being a writer in this country is worth, that literary fame and two bucks will get you on a Crosstown bus, and that only the vagaries of freelance journalism and my wife's job kept me out of the welfare office and off loading docks where I'd spent most of the last two decades scribbling stories on the backs of cigarette packs.

He wasn't listening any more than he had when I told him about Herman the German's tattoo. I could already hear him telling his salesman buddies over happy hour beer and nachos about "this writer I know," how, "we go back a long way," and he'd be, "bringing me on-side" as an investor in his latest pipe-dream. I made my excuses and he gave me his business card. It bore the logo of some financial services company whose office was a PO Box and whose number was a 1-800 line.

He scrawled his personal cell number on the back. I put it in my pocket after scanning it with a polite nod and gave him the number of a pub I'd been barred from as a result of a discussion about freedom of speech that ultimately involved police, paramedics and significant property damage. He wrote it down in his thick black leather Daytimer. I hoped the staff wouldn't remember me if he called.

## Herman the German

I got wine and a silk shirt for my wife and was heading for the doors at the other end of the mall to avoid a repeat encounter with Paul, when I passed a barbershop. Three under-employed barbers sat in their chairs swapping sections of the paper and I needed a haircut. The one who gave up his seat to me looked like the Bürgermeister of a small Bavarian town, complete with aldermanic paunch, Bismarck moustache and grey brush-cut. He complimented me on my army surplus sweater. He'd had one, "chust like it, after ze vor," he informed me in an accent thicker than a schnitzel.

In the back of my head, a penny dropped. At my sister's place a few months before, I'd heard her arguing with one of my teenage nephews who couldn't get a quick appointment with his usual stylist.

"Just go to the barbershop at the mall and get a haircut, for Christ sake!"

"But Mom ..." he whined. "I might get Herman the German..."

I'd had a quiet laugh to myself. Forty years on, kids were still calling some barber with a Mittel-European accent Herman the German. Now, once again, I had fallen into his hands. This Herman was too young to have worn *feldgrau*, but old enough for a little khaki uniform that wasn't the Boy Scouts. I enquired if he was from Germany or Austria.

"Osterreich, of course."

*Of course.* Intensity of nationalism occurs in inverse proportion to a country's size, strategic importance and access to open water. His indignation was slightly muted because I was a customer, after all. He busied himself tightening the sheet around my neck like a noose. I remarked that I found Austria very beautiful when I drove the Alpenstraße a few years ago.

In fact, my friend Ron Hyslop and I found it spooky, having driven up to Obersalzburg, Hitler's alpine holiday camp and planned final redoubt, simply because we were in the neighbourhood and who knew when we would be again? American Occupation Forces had built the Hotel General Walker, an R&R facility, on the site. Nothing was left of the chalets of the Reich-Meisters but the ruins of underground garages that once housed their gleaming black Mercedes. The Allies had bombed the place, just to let Hitler know they could and would. The craters were still there, deep depressions filled with neatly trimmed grass.

The view was oddly disappointing, a postcard of Tyrolean Alps too pretty to be beautiful, pure kitsch. Two beefy old men in loden jackets and *jaeger* hats avoided us, muttering to each other like heretic pilgrims in disguise visiting a ruined forbidden shrine. I made a point of asking them to take our picture with our camera. Politely, they did, but they didn't ask us to snap them with their Leica.

"I *valked* ze Alpenstraße ven I vas nineteen! Every kilometre!"

It was going to be that kind of conversation. If I mentioned the Rockies, Herman would prefer the Tyrolean Alps. I riffled through the local *North Shore News* looking for a neutral subject while Herman attacked my unkempt mop. An ad announced that a well-known seafood restaurant operating on the old Burrard Inlet ferry, moored at the foot of Lonsdale, had changed hands. We'd both eaten there and agreed the food was fit only for tourists. Herman nodded sagely as he whipped out the electric clippers and began to blitzkrieg my scalp.

"Ze liddle Chewish boy has zold out at last..."

I hesitated, thinking I might just have hair in my ears. The owner's name was obviously Greek. After a thoughtful moment I said so. Mirrored, Herman shook his head once, curtly dismissive. The walrus moustache spread slightly, masking a sneer.

"A liddle Chewish boy. Belief me, I know."

He tapped his nose with a finger and continued buzzing around my ears like a Stuka strafing a refugee column. Hair cascaded onto the blue apron covering my lap. I knew Salonika had once been the largest Jewish city in the world, but I also knew this family. I kept my voice flat, my face a mask in the opposing mirror.

"A friend of mine dated his daughter. They're Orthodox Greeks."

The electric clipper snapped off. Herman winked knowingly.

"Zey may zay so. Anyvay, he makes his money. Zose pipple alvays do..."

He worked his thumb and forefinger together in the universal gesture for dough, bread, moolah, cash, grease, *baksheesh*, *gelt*. It's a nasty gesture, lewd rubbing suggestive of masturbation. Having it demonstrated literally under my nose by fat fingers redolent of beer sausage and the pungent cologne affected by German men didn't make it any less so.

## Funny, I don't Look Jewish...

I realized this Herman the German wasn't going to believe me any more than Paul had believed me about the old Herman twenty years before. The human ability to continue to hold beliefs in the face of such trivial considerations as factual evidence no longer shocked or surprised me. What drove a wild hair up my ass was his assumption that I was either some bullet-headed bigot like himself, or that I would just sit there, smile and murmur politely in that all too Canadian fashion while he oozed his venom into my ear.

I'm not Jewish and I don't look it by any stretch of *Doktor Mengele's* skull tape-measure, but a lot of Jews don't 'look Jewish.' What if my best friend happened to be a Jew? Maybe a good neighbour, a respected teacher, a writer I knew and esteemed. Anyone I loved might coincidentally be a Jew. He didn't know me from Adam. I was just some guy who walked in from the mall, the anonymous air-conditioned agora, the post-modern *platz*. I could have been Simon Wiesenthal's nephew for all he knew, or a Mossad agent, since the Israelis had recently used forged Canadian passports to get close enough to an Islamic jihadist leader to punch his ticket permanently.

"My wife is Jewish. The mother of my children is a Jew."

The words were out of my mouth before I thought about them. If I hadn't just had the Paul-in-the-mall experience, maybe I would've done the Canadian thing, rolled with it, shrugged it off, paid for my haircut, got mad later and subjected my wife to a tirade of moral outrage over dinner. In fact, my wife is Canadian, of an Irish-Protestant father and an Australian, originally Austrian-Catholic maternal line. Being a writer of fiction, a liar by trade, has its perks. The abrupt and total silence that followed is one of them.

*ClipClipClipClipClipClipClip*.

Fastest and second worst haircut of my life. The old Herman's was worse only because he drew blood. I still have the scar on my left earlobe. When the sheet was whipped away, I stood up, lifted my jacket off the rack with a finger, grabbed my wine and my package and walked out without stopping at the cash register. I wanted to see if he'd follow me out into the mall bellowing, "Schtop, thief!" Maybe even *"Jude!"*

I had lied. That would diminish my credibility in court if I was charged with theft of services. I could've written up the proceedings for the *North Shore News* myself, casting him as a rabid anti-Semite, but making me look like the kind of mouth-foaming troll that spends all his time Twittering vicious rumours, usually about celebrities or politicians, trying to make a politically correct issue out of any innocuous remark to take some parasitic satisfaction from the mere reflection of fame.

As boys we had been as wrong as can be about our Herman, but fifty years later, in the early years of the new millennium, old Nazi war criminals were still being discovered living quietly in suburban Canadian neighbourhoods. Public opinion was divided between the "send them back to be hanged in their wheelchairs" crowd and those who argued that they had lived exemplary lives in Canada and would probably need a ramp to get to the gallows, so what was the point?

If I hadn't become a father late in life, I might have been willing to shrug the whole thing off as the bitter dregs of a previous century, better forgotten, if not forgiven, as we looked to a brighter future. But one night not long before I met Paul again and accidentally sat in the chair of the new Herman the German, I was idly watching one of those late re-runs of *The World at War* while reading a book, only half listening to Sir Laurence Olivier's ponderous narration. They were showing footage of the death camps I'd seen numerous times since high school history class; limp skeletal bodies bulldozed into pits, cold brick crematoria, obscene mounds of hair and teeth.

I looked up to see a still photo of people getting off cattle cars at Auschwitz, lined up on the platform clutching their pathetic personal bundles. Half those faces—the elderly, women and children—were minutes from death in the initial selection for the gas chambers. For the first time, all I saw were the faces of the children, so like the faces of my own sleeping safely upstairs. They weren't screaming or crying. They glowed with a terrible radiant innocence from the small silent screen; trusting, incapable of imagining that adults, *grown-ups*, were about to exterminate them like vermin, that their small bodies, each containing myriad possible human futures, would soon be incinerated like so much garbage at a landfill.

So Herman the German picked the wrong time to get in my face. I was up for a polka with the RCMP and the Human Rights Commission if he was. But when I looked over my shoulder he was giving his fellow barbers the Viennese shrug, already passing me off as one of those loose cannons every barber, bartender and cab driver has to put up with in a day. He'd wanted to share his secret hate with someone, but not with the world.

In the car, I took the long way home, along the street where our Herman's house had been. A new house had been built on the property and already recently renovated. It had nice little half-bay windows and a design-gesture of a front porch crowded with white plastic deck furniture. The siding was low maintenance pastel vinyl. The curtains were cheerful and the front steps would satisfy a spirit-level. A young man was mowing the small lawn, perfect as a putting green. A lovely young woman solicitously attended its border of pansies and nasturtiums with polished brass trowels and watering-cans. A picture-perfect blond baby lolled nearby in a three-wheel Gore-Tex stroller that cost half as much as my car.

They looked up at my idling car, faces bland, innocently unhistorical. I hit the gas and drove off before they reported my plates, not maliciously, but prudently, as a possibly suspicious character Neighbourhood Watch should know about. Checking my fresh-out-of-prison haircut in the rear-view mirror, I remembered that when I was a kid and men got their hair cut every Saturday, my Dad used to say that the difference between a bad haircut and a good haircut was six days. Sometimes, it's longer.

FIVE

# The Skin Trade

"You *what?*"

"I got a tattoo, Mom."

"Oh, my God... *why?*"

This exchange between my sister and her twenty-year-old son went pretty much tune and verse as it did with my Mom and me twenty years before. He also got a value-added rerun of what I got from his Grandmother, since two decades have done zip to blunt her wits or tongue. It's how this conversation goes between mothers and sons, or daughters, and has for a millennium.

Models of maternal tolerance, my mother and sister chose their battles with their children with care. They declined skirmishes over dress or length and colour of hair. But in our culture, practices like piercing and tattooing now described as body modification provoke a womb-clench of horror in a mother, who responds instinctively to the mutilation of the flesh of her child, regardless of current age. You say: *Mom, I got a tattoo.*

Your mother hears: *Remember that impossibly silky skin and the delicate soporific scent new-born babies exude? I paid a criminal thug to use dirty needles to carve a hideously tacky picture and the name of some diseased slut into it with permanent ink.*

*Why? Because it's not your baby's cherubic sexless dependent little body anymore. It's a grown-up body. My body. By getting a tattoo, I claim my body as my own.*

Nobody ever says this. The young and recently-illustrated mumble vague rationales, "I think it looks cool... I'm old enough..." to skirt a truth as painful as it is liberating. We are our selves, separate from the bodies that created us; unique and alone.

John Gray titled his irreverent 1994 history of tattooing *I Love Mom* as a tribute to what is ironically the English word most commonly inked into human skin. Military medics for all armies unofficially report the last word uttered by most dying servicemen is "Mother." When soldiers and sailors get it tattooed on a forearm or bicep they're going on record in case, as happens often enough, they don't get a chance to say anything at all.

Their mothers still would not approve.

## The Unillustrated Man

Spring of 1981 is rainy and cold. The streets east of Main in Vancouver are a moody Impressionist watercolour of grey and amber bricks congealed into clumsy shapes pretending to be buildings. Lit by a diffused acetylene glow, the sky reflects weakly in gutters and not at all in windows unwashed for decades. The strongest colours are prismatic sheens of motor oil spreading faint rainbows on worn slick cobblestones and crumbly asphalt. Standing outside the low narrow storefront of Star Tattoo, the wide collar of my pea jacket turned up, its slash pockets full of my fists, I study the gaudy illustrations in the window. They are so much more vivid and provocatively symbolic than anything in the surrounding cityscape. I try to look like some down-and-out *boulevardier* merely piqued by the aesthetic contrast they offer to the monochrome squalor of the neighbourhood.

It's a pose. I'm here to get a tattoo.

Few people who limp along the heaved sidewalk in the hunched seclusion of hoods and umbrellas show any interest in my whimsical "To be or not to be tattooed?" posturing. Well, I'll show them I'm not just some punk from the suburbs flirting with the idea to *epater les parents*. I will get a tattoo, dammit. Right now. A bell attached to the door frame of the shop tinkles cheaply. It tolls for me.

I am alone in the tiny brightly lit foyer whose walls glow with images in over-brilliant inks. Dragons, pythons and panthers writhe among arrow and dagger pierced hearts bleeding in an abundance that would gratify an Aztec priest. A beaded curtain cloaking the doorway to a back room is parted by the head of the biggest Doberman Pinscher I've ever locked eyes with.

"I hope you're not Pavlov's dog," I croak as soothingly as I can with a suddenly arid tongue.

## Warm art

Tattooing had enjoyed a renaissance in the decade before I stepped through the door and rang the Dobie dinner-bell. In the late 1960s hippies started getting inked with non-traditional designs, rainbows, butterflies and peace symbols and tattoos began being described as Warm Art. Lovers got tattoos on parts of the body not normally displayed, a mark of intimacy and commitment as indelible as the ink, in theory. Two decades later, comedienne Roseanne Barr and husband Tom Arnold annihilated the cachet of this practice by having each others names tattooed on their landscape-of-lard butts and showing them off at the merest provocation: an example of what's meant by the phrase *too much of a good thing*.

In 1981, many people still claimed to be disgusted by tattoos, associating them with convicts, drunk sailors, carnivals and seedy waterfront go-downs where irresponsible young men fortified with liquid guts undergo deliberate mutilations in unsanitary conditions in a *machismo*-proving ritual on dares by their peers. Tattooing is still illegal in some parts of the United States. Tattooing the hands or face, public parts of the body, is often prohibited even where body tattooing is permitted. Jailhouse tattoos on the hands, like the words Hate and Love the demented preacher played by Robert Mitchum in *Night of the Hunter* has tattooed on his fingers, are the sign of the self-proclaimed social outcast, the Mark of Cain.

The word comes from the Polynesian *tatau*, meaning "the result of tapping or striking." Captain Cook recorded it as "tattow," probably because he knew he'd have to explain the permanent heathen decorations his sailors brought home as souvenirs. His third Pacific voyage in 1776 marked European re-discovery of an art virtually stamped out by the rise of the Roman Catholic Church from the ashes of the Empire. Tattoos had religious and social import in pagan cultures, so the Church banned the visible manifestation of an order it meant to supplant. Suppressed in Europe, the art survived in outlying areas where the grip of the Church was too tenuous for a stranglehold.

Synchronicity: in *The White Goddess* Robert Graves notes that pre-Christian Celtic sea-farers often had a blue star tattooed on the palm, or between the thumb and forefinger on the back of the hand, as a charm against drowning. An ancient mariner we called Tex because of his big Stetson used to hang around the North Vancouver waterfront. Beside him on a bus one day when he grabbed the stanchion to get off, my eye was caught by a faded blue star tattooed between the thumb and forefinger of his right hand. Seeing that star rippled by wrinkles of living flesh was like finding an archaic manuscript in the pages of a pulp novel or kicking a stone and turning up an ancient wounded skull. Was that the reason I drifted around the eastside past a number of tattoo parlours and finally stopped in front of one called Star Tattoo?

## 1) Cleaning and shaving the area

"Don't mind him. He won't hurt you unless you try to hurt me."

The Doberman emits a low growl of reluctant confirmation.

She is about five feet tall, might weigh ninety pounds in a damp towel. Long straight hair falls to hips that are barely a gesture. Her jeans would fit a twelve-year-old boy, but no boy would fill that tight t-shirt so unequivocally. The dog has his work cut out for him, but seems equal to the job. He sniffs my offered hand as if it might contain a cheeseburger, or be an acceptable substitute.

"You want a tattoo?"

I nod.

"Know what you want?"

I nod again.

"This way."

In the back room, she invites me to sit in a surprisingly modern contoured reclining chair my dentist might envy. The Doberman positions himself to my right and sits in an attitude of unnerving alertness, clocking the distance between his incisors and my jugular.

"Take off your jacket and shirt."

Piercing and more extreme rituals of cutting with razors are erotic aspects of sadomasochistic fetish cults populated by people who just don't find Saturday night at a sports bar full of beer-maddened jocks sexy enough. The sexual subtext of tattooing is more obvious now that women routinely expose private parts of their bodies to total strangers and allow themselves to be penetrated with needles that ejaculate permanent ink.

I am very aware I am taking off my shirt for an attractive strange young woman. So is the Doberman, who murmurs appreciation at having his target area widened. Lying back in the chair, I explain I want a single rose tattooed above my heart. She offers me a bouquet of small rose patterns. Embarrassed, I pick one at random, like a dork boyfriend choosing a single bloom at a florist on Valentine's Day.

Brusquely she runs a razor over the area, dabs it cool with alcohol and spreads the template on my chest. She picks up her needle gun. It emits a low insect buzz, like barber clippers or a vibrator. Then she straddles me and seats herself firmly on my lap. I'd pay serious money to have a picture of my face at that moment.

"Am I too heavy?"

As if considering an engineering problem, I take a moment to carefully weigh the light but exquisite pressure her ass, thighs and pubic arch are exerting on my confined groin.

"Has any guy ever answered *yes* to that question?"

She smiles innocently.

"No. They never have."

"Didn't think so."

Snugging her denimed butt and crotch comfortably into mine, she leans forward. Her long brown hair brushes the taut skin of my exposed belly like a warm breeze. Every remaining hair on my body stands to attention.

"This is going to hurt."

Not kidding, she pushes the needle-gun down, piercing my skin. The closest thing to it I'd felt before was getting a wasp trapped in my shirt one summer. It stung me repeatedly in the same small area before I could shake it out and stomp on it twenty or thirty times.

## 2) Prepare a stencil of the design

Random facts to think about to take your mind off the pain while getting a tattoo:

Primitive tattooing instruments are sometimes found at sites of Neolithic cave paintings.

Certain ancient Egyptian mummies, all women, have tattoos preserved with their skin. Egyptian ladies may not have spent quite as much at the cosmetician as previously thought, but used tattoos as a form of permanent makeup.

In 1948 the two-thousand-year-old heavily tattooed body of a Scythian chief was discovered in the Altai region of the former Soviet Union.

The ancient Incas practised the art, as did the Chinese when Marco Polo dropped in.

In 54 B.C. Julius Caesar invaded Britain and recorded in his *Commentaries* that the natives painted their bodies blue. They actually tattooed their bodies with blue woad, a practice that lingered in outlying areas until recently, e.g. the star tattoo I saw on Tex's hand.

The full body tattoo is making a comeback in some traditional Polynesian societies. In New Zealand, young Maori get traditional facial tattoos to defiantly proclaim their cultural resurgence in post-colonial society.

Full body tattooing achieved its finest expression in feudal Japan. Samurai nobles, fearing erosion of traditional order by an increasingly wealthy middle class, made it a crime for any but the nobles to wear jewels and fine robes. The middle class retaliated by getting gorgeous body-suit tattoos, leaving only the hands and feet unmarked. Taking years to complete, their incomparable complexity and colouration turns the wearer into a kind of living silk scroll or screen. Post World War II, this tradition is perpetuated by another nouveau riche sub-culture, the *yakuza*, gangsters of Japanese organized crime.

Like crude jailhouse tattoos acquired by prison inmates in our culture or the teardrop cheek tattoo awarded to gang-bangers when they make their first kill, most tattoos are a permanent badge of belonging to an *out-caste*. They illustrate the motto, "Once in, never out," reinforcing gang solidarity. A tattoo is a membership card that can't be torn up, revoked only by death. Once the ink is in your skin, you can't wash it off and be "yourself" again.

A tattoo transforms you into someone else.

Both Orthodox Jews and the Catholic Church forbid tattooing on grounds that Man is made "in the image of God," thus altering the body is desecrating the image of God. Judaism retains particular prohibitions against tattoos. With my friend, novelist Martin Cohen, one afternoon, picking up his son from summer camp, I can't help noting how many kids sport pierced ears, navels, eyebrows.

A tolerant orthodox Rabbi, Martin explains, "They use the piercing thing to push the Law without actually breaking it. I tell parents, 'A nose-ring you can live with for a few years,' but we get our share of crazies. I once had a guy come to my office insisting he wanted to convert to Judaism. After talking to him, I concluded he was somewhat unbalanced and suggested he take more time to think it over. Suddenly he says, 'But Rabbi, what should I do about *this*?' He rips open his shirt to reveal he has JHWH, the acronym of God, tattooed in letters of fire inside a pentagram covering his whole chest. I managed to remain calm while I told him, '*That* may be a problem.'"

## 3) Inking the outline

Rills of bright red blood well up and run down my chest. She wipes them away with a gauze pad, swabbing as she continues to sting me like a bee worrying a flower, a red rose she seems to be drawing pollen from and pollinating all in one sanguinary and sexual act. She doesn't shift her hips, much less grind in any overt way. I am intensely aware that only a few layers of thin cotton separate our genitals, yet neither of us is getting damp in that area. We are both focused on the small raw patch of skin above my heart.

"How did you learn to do this?"

She shrugs, keeps needling me.

"My boyfriend taught me. He's a biker and a tattooist. The dog's his idea. Figures it'll protect me. This isn't a great neighbourhood."

"I noticed the *ambiance* is a bit downmarket."

"Yeah, well, there're a lot of real creeps around here. Sometimes they wander in and get ideas..."

"Not for long, I guess."

"Not so far."

I can't help staring at the spot where our jeans seem to blend into each other. The view is impeded slightly by the leather holster of a Buck clasp knife. She notices where I am looking.

"That keeps the freaks off too. But it's mainly the dog. The idea of trying to not get stabbed while a savage dog is chewing your dick off is more than most guys who wander in here can deal with."

"Ever had to pull it?"

"Once or twice. Word gets around you don't take any shit."

That I knew from experience, but talking distracts me from the fact that my chest is being exquisitely flayed.

"Keep still. I have to ink the petals."
I keep still.
So does she.
So does the Doberman.

We are a tableau of blood and sublimated sex in a small quiet room; surrounded by a world of implicit and explicit violence, yet oddly serene. Watching my blood ooze out from under the humming needle, fists clenched, refusing to wince or cry out, I know the euphoria of power, of self-control. With a blood oath, I am swearing I am someone who can take it. In the grand scheme of things, being able to take it without whining is the Holy Grail of tough. It's why tattooing is a feature of coming-of-age rituals, for both boys and girls, in so many societies.

A tattoo is a stylized scar, a product of deliberate ritual mutilation, symbol of something you are meant to remember, not an accident to be forgotten. Lots of boys can inflict pain, yet bullies are often the first to fold when they have to endure it. They're no use to a warrior or hunter society. Women know a girl who will bear children and help other women bear theirs can't be skittish about blood and pain. A tattoo marks you as someone who will stand up and take it when things get tough, as they surely will.

## 4) Colouring and Shading

A tattoo can signify anything, but it always signifies *something*. The image may have overt resonance, like the stern of a sinking ship a sailor I know has on his bicep above a scroll bearing the bannered legend "Sailors Grave." He got it after serving on a ship wrecked in the Red Sea. The tattoo is a souvenir of survival, a reminder that no matter what misfortune blights his life, he's been in a worse jackpot, doing the backstroke in a sea famous for the ravenous appetite of its resident sharks.

Men get regimental or corps tattoos when they join the armed forces or coded tattoos when committed to prison because both experiences involve surrendering personal will and moral judgement to an institutional order. Tattoos are the institutionalized individual's way of "taking back the body," while at the same time confirming solidarity with fellow inmates, a blood oath that cements the fraternity of shared suffering.

Anorexics, body-builders, and suicides understand that true power begins and ends with the body. The image tattooed doesn't matter; a panther or naked woman or a heart pierced by a dagger bearing the name of a girl who doesn't remember yours. Its only purpose may be proving to yourself you're brave enough to endure the experience of getting it. But all tattoos ultimately have the same purpose: re-possession of the body by deliberate alteration.

Tattoos, pierced eyebrows, lips and tongues with decorative studs currently popular among young adults are a revolutionary manifesto in altered flesh. They are a public and permanent expression of a commitment to live outside the corporate cultural status quo. Unlike sixties hippies, whose passive uncut hair meant they could literally go 'straight' from the barber into real estate or junk bond sales, the new generation of rebels get tattoos and piercings that exclude them from socially acceptable public roles unless they're willing to undergo reconstructive surgery.

## 5) Care of the Tattoo While It Heals

Thirty ears ago, I wasn't looking to get a manifesto inked on my chest. I chose to bear a rose on an inconspicuous part of my body because that flower has scattered its symbolic petals from the medieval *Romaunt de la Rose* to the wacky mysticism of the Rosicrucians, to Tennesee Williams' play *The Rose Tattoo*. At the time, I felt like Lancelot from the *Morte d'Arthur*; a knight whose courage in combat counts for nothing in the Grail quest because his flawed character plays falsely with every woman who loves him. My history is less mythic.

I hadn't been getting along with a girl I was living with and a female co-worker remarked on it over drinks in the pub. Defensive, I denied it until my festering hostility toward my girlfriend was spewing out so obviously even I could see it. Drunken argument ended with us fucking frantically on a flight of stairs, an act I've never repeated, on stairs, at least. Stricken with guilt, I married the girlfriend I'd betrayed in a hasty civil ceremony. A week later I was fucking my co-worker again—*sans escaliers*—a total and utter *asshole*.

In retrospect, I tell myself that this makes no less sense than other illicit affairs I've observed. At the time I felt I was crossing the border of sanity with a fake passport. Loathing the self who'd got me into a bind where no matter what I did, I was in the wrong, I withdrew from both women. After a few weeks of sulking silence and isolation, I put on my pea jacket, flipped up the collar and jumped a bus to the Downtown Eastside streets where I used to drink Silex coffee in neon cafes and talk to whoever would talk to me, walk cold sidewalks with no destination, and duck out of the wind in recessed doorways like long gone Captain Ted's Tattoo Parlour to meditate on the possibilities of flesh as garishly symbolic as a Tibetan Buddhist scroll through windows tinted by time, grime, and cigarette smoke.

"Am I done?"

"You're done."

She tapes a gauze pad over the gaudy bloody rose on my chest and takes my money. In lieu of change she hands me a cheaply printed page of instructions for the care of my tattoo as it heals. I stuff it in the pocket of my pea jacket as I shrug it on over my loosely buttoned shirt, mindful of the tender spot over my heart.
"Thanks."
"Uh...you're welcome."

There isn't anything else to say. She begins dismantling her needle gun into an enamel kidney dish of disinfectant. The Doberman escorts me through the bead curtain and out of the shop. As I close the door behind me, the bell tinkles like the warning clarion of a plague-cart. I step into a day disintegrating into night. Buildings dissolve, neon signs free-float in the darkness and skeins of cold rain ripple briefly under streetlights. I feel like I should have at least asked her to tell me her name. She drew my blood, marked my skin for life, altered me, literally changed my self-image, for as long as forever is.

Why? For her, it was an impersonal act. Like a whore, or shaman, (the simile I prefer), she performed a ritual service as professionally as a rabbinical *mohel*. Its significance was specific to me, generic to her. I chose to be tattooed, to alter my body. I chose the design. If I turn up dead in a ditch, that thirty-year-old tattoo will be among the identifying marks in a police forensic report.

## 6) Prophylaxis

My tattoo is an *aide memoire*, prophylaxis against personal historical revisionism. We lie to ourselves every day, starting with the rationale for getting out of bed in the morning. But every time I put on or take off my shirt, step in or out of the shower, shave or get ready to go out into the world, my tattoo is there in the mirror, saying what I might conveniently forget without that visual cue: "You may truly be a vicious man, but you don't have to *act* like one. Every day, when you see the sign of the rose in your skin, you can choose between the true and false in yourself, between love and hate, between doing good or doing harm, if only just for this one day."

Psychobabblers and positivist mantra-peddlers of the self-help industry call this a daily affirmation, albeit of the flesh rather than the word. Yet that's what my tattoo is there to subvert. Seeing it in the mirror prevents me from looking myself in the eye every morning and telling myself what a great guy I am and how I'm getting grander by the minute. My tattoo reminds me that at heart I'm still a selfish, cruel man who, if he's very mindful and tries very hard, might get through the day without behaving like one and be able to enjoy the sleep of the just for a few hours.

After more than three decades, my tattoo has faded into the kind of indefinite smudge that aging skin makes of Warm Art, a degradation inevitable as death, something tattooists don't mention to their customers. But like a prayer learned by rote, I no longer require the precise lineaments to recall its message.

"You could get that re-inked, you know," multiple-pierced and illustrated young people at the community pool tell me when we get to comparing personal insignia in the big communal hot tub after dutifully swimming our laps.

Yeah, I could. I could also get it surgically removed or burned off with a laser. I don't need or want to. Its power as the symbol of an act of contrition, an act of faith, an oath consecrated with my blood, isn't diminished by sharing my descent toward inevitable decrepitude and death. My tattoo has aged with me, been absorbed deeper into the universal part of me unrecognizable to others, what the religiously-minded might call my soul. As it decays into a Rorschach blot, it is more vivid to me now than the day it erupted from my flesh and wrote itself in blood on my body like some mystical graffito. It has evolved from the bright, stylized pattern of an archetypal symbol into a unique hieroglyph of blurred ink; my secret signature, the ideograph of my true name in this world.

SIX

# Raincity Style

And God said unto Noah, *"How's yer boat comin' along?"* Or words to that effect. Had Noah lived on the Wet Coast of British Columbia, his reaction to Jehovah's rant about the sinfulness of the world and threats of The Great Flood and all would likely have been more phlegmatic.

"Only forty days and forty nights? Shit, last year she rained a full eight weeks without a let-up. Guess I better get another tarp over the friggin' boat, so she don't get more rot in the rails and transom..."

Had the Ark been built hereabouts, it would, like many a ship of dreams, still be on cradles in some marina dry-land storage yard, draped like a circus tent, with a woodstove installed on the afterdeck and a bar fridge powered by a granny knot of extension cords illegally tapped into the local hydro line, accessed by a shaky gangway of jury-rigged ladders and stairs made of scrounged lumber. A wheel-less gypsy caravan, a ship out of water, a thing between two worlds, reeking of female-repellent resins, oils, thinners and paint—sanctuary for any male in need of a place to hang out, play a few hands of crib and shoot the proverbial shit with the excuse of workin' on the boat.

On this ark, no wildlife would survive but the malodorous dog sleeping under the galley table, fed on the same canned chili, injected with bottled hot sauce, as the card-playing Argonauts and emitting farts of equally spectacular toxicity. Noah's dove would have been savaged by pirate gulls that streak the tarps with excreted leftover fish 'n' chips from the marina cafe. If it miraculously escaped and returned with an olive branch, some poor bastard would only have to put on his raingear and slog up to Jack the Bootlegger's for enough gin to decently marinate the bloody things.

Working on the boat is a return to those times when human beings sought shelter from bad weather, settled into a cosy cave with the Neolithic equivalent of a few ales, got out the mammoth-ivory Scrabble tiles to spell out some simple grunts and sensibly waited for it to stop. If it was the rainy season, on the B.C. coast this could take awhile, which may explain why local indigenous cultures were so richly layered and complex. They had lots of time to buff up their dancing, carving, singing, storytelling, and weaving cedar bark into capes and conical hats to keep the rain off. An anthropologist studying contemporary west coast culture would describe rain gear as our "distinctive regional costume."

Like the elders of this and every other place, we wear our history every day. Fashionable or merely faddish, clothes have ancestors, family trees as complex as our own, the result of millennia of historical and cultural influences. But whether you slip into a grass skirt, tie a robe or rug up in furs, the dominant influence on your choice of ensemble for the day is likely to be the weather where you live.

## Not Fit for Man Nor Beast

The Industrial Revolution promoted the perverse idea that people ought to get out of warm dry beds and go to work at the same time every day, even on days when any less rational animal would sensibly curl up in its warm farty den for an extended snooze. This unnatural behaviour was essential to maintain predictable levels of manufactured production, but completely at odds with traditional, seasonal patterns of agrarian labour and life. Understandably, the IR channelled a good deal of creative energy into products that would enable and encourage workers to accept, if not embrace, the concept of a workday that was not seasonally or meteorologically determined. The alarm clock, the raincoat, waterproof footwear, the umbrella, and public transportation—all exist in defiance of the amount of common sense possessed by a domestic cat, whose brain may be the size of a hazelnut but is still smart enough to stay in out of the rain and shit in your shoe if you haven't cleaned its litter-box lately.

The discovery of India-rubber, (*caoutchouc*), by French explorers in the 1700s was initially a dud. Like Silly Putty or Flubber, it was marvellous, except that nobody could figure out what to do with it in anything resembling a practical or profitable application. In 1770, a Dr. Priestly discovered it would rub out lead pencil marks, making corrections a miserable reality for elementary school students, but the tropical forests of the misnamed Indies of the New World seemed like a hell of a long way to go for an eraser.

Early in the 1830s, Charles Macintosh devised a process for impregnating fabric with India-rubber to create "waterproof" clothing. Despite the British climate, which would seem to make such apparel *de rigeur* year round, his invention was only a limited success. The drawback was the notoriously anti-social odour, a side effect of the process, produced by the garments that came to bear his name. A diarist of the time observed: "Complaints were made that the Macintosh is becoming a troublesome thing in Town from the difficulty of their being admitted to an omnibus on account of the offensive stench which they emit." Obviously the writer had yet to ride a Vancouver omnibus on which dozens of freshly applied perfumes, colognes, after-shaves, and deodorants compete with the mineral bouquet of early edition printers ink for the attention of one's allergic sensors.

Inventor's names often stick to things long after the product has evolved. The overly aromatic rubber capes Macintosh developed were soon eclipsed, yet "Mac" is still widely used in England to describe any type of raincoat. Sometimes the inventor's identity is eclipsed by the name of the person who commissions the object, like the Wellington Boot. The English, as well as pseudo-Brit Canadians, still call rubber boots "Wellies," yet the boot that bears his name bears no resemblance to the one the Duke commissioned from his now forgotten boot-maker during the Napoleonic Wars.

On campaign, English officers customarily wore riding boots. Stiff, knee-high leather toe-crushers, usually spurred. Getting in or out of them required effort and assistance. What Wellington wanted after a day in the saddle was to get his dogs out of those bloody things and into something loose, dry and comfortable as quickly as possible. Unfortunately he travelled with 50,000 or so other guys and a lot of horses who could transform an idyllic meadow into a stinking bog of gluey mud and mixed excrement in about ten minutes. A gentleman could hardly swan about wearing dancing pumps in that kind of shite, so the Duke commissioned a "camp boot" of loose fit, reaching halfway up the calf, which resembles the infamous German jack-boot. One observer actually reported that the Duke wore "Hessian boots," probably borrowed from one of the soldiers from Hesse who served in the British Army under Hanoverian kings.

Called Engineers Boots in the 1950s, black leather versions of the jack-boot known as dispatch rider boots or biker boots are more legitimate descendants of the original Wellington than the black rubber things that now bear the Duke's illustrious name. The latter are "gumboots," the professional footwear of fishermen and sailors, not soldiers. Crews of Canada's insanely brave submarine-hunting corvettes in World War II proudly called themselves "The Gumboot Navy." Rubber boots have been the footwear of farmers, gardeners, and puddle-jumping kids for generations.

## The Goodyear Imp

The "gumboot" is where Charles Macintosh and the Duke's anonymous boot-maker come together, with help from Charles Goodyear, who developed the process known as vulcanizing in 1839. This process stabilized rubber for almost limitless applications and made it viable for clothes and footwear; the first practical, socially acceptable use of rubber technology. It would also be used to make condoms, an application unmentionable at the time.

Goodyear made boots and over-shoes of rubber and later made the first widespread use of a revolutionary zip-fastener, then still too cumbersome to be used in clothing. These were the galoshes still popular in the 1950s among white-collar office workers, who wore them over their oxfords. Galoshes were a squalid species of footwear, impossible to wear with anything resembling *elan*.

When I was a kid, gumboots offered the same colour options as the original Model A Ford; any colour you wanted so long as it was black. They were footwear as democratic as the wooden *sabot* of French workers, whose habit of tossing one into the gears of the mill on hung-over Mondays during the Industrial Revolution is the root of our word *sabotage*. We folded the tops of our red-soled black gumboots down into wide reverse cuffs, imitating musketeers and pirates, achieving a degree of *panache* that caused those forced into galoshes by their mothers to hide their feet under the back seats of the school bus in shame.

For those who don't believe black accessorizes with everything, Wellies now come in designer colours. Green seems to be favoured by the kind of West Vancouver colonial relics who practise their English accents while pruning the roses. You can still get basic black, right down to the rust-coloured soles, though most are badly made in formerly Communist east European republics. That's something you may want to factor into that incredibly cheap vacation package at Club Med Bratislava you just booked on the internet. Still, if Napoleon's troops had gumboots at Waterloo, where thick mud from a heavy rainstorm the night before affected the outcome of the battle, they'd be called "Boneys" today.

Fluorescent yellow has become the default colour for gear worn by fishermen and outside workers in situations where your life may depend on your degree of visibility in weather not fit for man nor beast. Even makers of deluxe yacht wear favour yellow. It lends a rakish air to sailors who need protection on rough days in the wet bar of a sixty-foot motorboat. My anthropologist brother Phil has noted the popularity of the "hi-viz" vest, a mesh of orange or lime green crossed with fluorescent yellow stripes, as casual wear in Australia among young men keen to identify as serious working blokes. But it's the black or olive drab gear worn by loggers and construction workers that comes closest to Macintosh's originals.

It always reminds me of Ralph Cramden's sidekick in *The Honeymooners*, Ed Norton, who worked in the New York sewers—too obviously proletarian for the suburban gardener or weekend warrior class. Of course, the best place for any and all foul weather gear is the mudroom, pegged above and dripping into the gumboots, while rain rattles against the windows and you burrow into the couch under a crotchet afghan, cradling a good book, listening to Doc Watson on the stereo purring, "Let it rain, let it pour... Let it rain a whole lot more... 'cause I've got them Deep River Blues...

## You Can Leave Your Hat On

Back when early hominids began walking upright, Alan Fotheringham noted in a column in the *Vancouver Sun* that while a climate of near-perpetual rain caused Englishmen to evolve opposable thumbs to carry an umbrella, men in the 'California of Canada' refused to wear even the simplest head-covering in the face of equally hostile meteorology. The reason is as obvious as the hat on your head.

Canada's culturally distinctive headgear is the toque, a knitted cap favoured by Quebecois voyageurs who manually powered the big brigade canoes and York boats of the fur-trading Hudson's Bay and Northwest Companies. The toque's notable characteristics are flaccid shapelessness reminiscent of a used condom and luridly clashing colour combinations. It has the effect of making even a member of Mensa look like the kind of dude who has his bus pass pinned to his lapel and a card in his pocket with phone numbers of minders who'll collect him when he becomes a nuisance. In a sense, it's still the hat of voyageurs, since every certifiable wingnut wandering urban public transit systems wears one.

The other dim bulbs suckered into powering those fur brigade boats with their backs were Scots, who sported tams, a sort of knitted beige beret that makes the wearer look like he or she has a slab of cold porridge stuck in their hair. The urban cowboys of Calgary and Edmonton with their black or white ten-gallon rivalry are more stylish and more sensible. Big Stetsons are vulnerable to wind—and nothing looks as foolish as a man chasing his hat in a high wind—but they do shed rain and snow well off your noggin and shoulders and keep the 35% of body heat lost by a hatless person where it belongs.

It only took me forty-five years to figure this out, which may say something about the brain-softening effects of growing up in a temperate rainforest. I had to go to Alice Springs in the Northern Territories of Australia, a beer oasis located more or less in the middle of half a dozen very large deserts, before the penny dropped out of the mucus. Even in the so-called spring, if you walk around The Alice bareheaded your brain will poach in your skull during the short stagger between pubs.

I asked one of the many khaki-clad Crocodile Dundee impersonators who pass as tour guides what locals do in the blast furnace Outback summer, when the Red Centre shuts down for fear temperatures will cause the heads or hearts of non-acclimatized tourists to spontaneously explode.

"Can't answer for the rest of the mob," he said, "But I sit naked on a cement floor with a wet towel wrapped around moy fackin' head in front of an open fridge and toss tins of Vic Bitter down moy fackin' neck non-stop."

Sounded like a lifestyle to me, so I bought myself the quintessential Aussie hat, an Akubra Stockman, worn by *The Man from Snowy River*. After fifteen years of keeping everything from sun to snow and hail off my head, it developed a small hole worn by my thumb and forefinger pinching the point of the crown. Otherwise, it looked exactly like it did when I tried it on in the shop and admired the Indiana Jones clone who winked back at me.

The Akubra, I soon discovered, is a hat you earn the right to wear. First night out, at a winery dinner, I politely placed it, brim down, on the table. After a few minutes, during which he sussed I was a tourist because I ordered medallions of kangaroo in a red wine sauce—a dish our waitress cheerfully described as road-kill—an older man with the permanent sunburn of a seasoned territorial reached over from the next table, excused himself and gently turned my hat over to rest on the crown. Touching another man's hat is a firearms matter in some parts of the world. Had I been Australian, some tall poppy Sydney-sider on a patronizing tour of the country Beyond the Black Stump, he probably wouldn't have bothered.

"Spoils the brim," he whispered with an apologetic smile. Instantly I saw what he meant. Laying the hat on flat surfaces brim-down spoils the raffish rain-displacing rake. I was grateful to him, not only for stopping me from ruining an expensive hat, but for a glimpse into the spirit of the Australian pioneer. Placing my hat on the table the wrong way was an affront to his most basic values. It must've been driving him off his dinner to see a fine hat treated in such an ignorant abusive manner, yet his correction of my *gaffe* was gentle and polite.

The frontier isn't a line on a map. It's a nebulous region defined more by attitude than GPS coordinates. Not always frugal, but ever economical, it's a state of mind that values the simplest things because of the long distances they have to come, or the great effort involved in producing them, to make life on the margins of civilisation endurable. In the Outback, a good hat is not a fashion statement. It has travelled a long way to save your life where lack of one can end it quickly. Such an item deserves to be treated with respect, like a tool kept sharp even in the box, or a gun cleaned and oiled in the rack.

## Under My Umbrella

*"Bus stop, wet day, she's there, I say, "Please share my umbrella..."*
—The Hollies

Had The Hollies been a West Coast band, their sixties hit would have had slightly different lyrics. For starters, she would have been the one with the foresight to carry an umbrella and it would probably be one of those neat fold-up Knirps units that popped up like mushrooms the decade that song hit the charts. West Coast men, who wouldn't don a hat in a hailstorm for fear of diluting their testosterone, would rather wear eye shadow than carry something as unspeakably effete as an umbrella.

The compact candy-cane collapsible units of the Sixties were the first major technical innovation in umbrella manufacture in over a century, a refining tweak on a basic design that hasn't changed in about four thousand years. Umbrellas are instantly recognizable in ancient Egyptian and Assyrian bas-relief—circular canopies supported by spokes radiating from a central shaft.

Technically, those venerable brollies are parasols, providing protection from brain-boiling sun, not rain. Peripatetic ancient Greeks brought the parasol to Europe. Romans, who loved everything about Greece, except its politics, were the first Europeans to use the umbrella to keep their heads cool in the line-up for Coliseum tickets. The Chinese naturally claim to have invented the umbrella when Adam's bike had training-wheels. Since they developed printing, silk, gunpowder, and pasta while we were still poking each other with blunt sticks, it's reasonable to assume they'd figure out a coating of wax on a paper parasol would create serviceable temporary shelter from a squall.

Like most niceties of civilised life, the umbrella folded up during the Dark Ages, to re-open in Italy during the Renaissance. So powerful was the Mediterranean cultural influence that the English couldn't be bothered to coin a word for the thing. Umbrella comes straight from Italian, "a little shade," and its Latin root, umbra (shade/shadow), as if Londoners ever had cause to fear sunstroke. The French, more sensitive to semantic and meteorological shades of meaning, took the trouble to distinguish a *parasol* from a *parapluie*.

## Over My Head

Then, as in the ancient world, the umbrella was often a symbol of high office, restricted to nobles and clergy who could afford to employ flunkies to stand around holding heavy clumsy things over the exalted noggins of Princes, Cardinals, and Doges. But a device so simple and practical couldn't be kept from the common people indefinitely. By the 16th and 17th centuries, the umbrella had come into wide use in northern Europe for reasons obvious to anyone who has ever been there on a summer holiday.

Mentioned by Swift ("A Description of a City Shower", 1710), the umbrella in England was initially an item of exclusively feminine fashion, until stubbornly popularized by Persian traveller Jonas Hanway, (1712-1786), who knew better than to care what he looked like as long as he was out of the English weather. Teased by street urchins and persecuted by coachmen, who saw umbrellas as a threat to their trade and deliberately drove through gutters to splash him, (their descendants work for Metro Transit), Hanway toted a brolly through London for three decades and lived to see his foresight vindicated. By the time he died, the umbrella no longer carried the stigmas of effeminacy or pedestrianism (being too poor to afford a carriage). It had become a standard accoutrement of the English gentleman, often called a "Hanway."

Umbrellists were a favourite subject of London's satirical pamphleteers, who mocked the fashions of the day. Specimens of "The Twirler" and "The Fencer" are still among us and have to be treated with the pedestrian equivalent of defensive driving on buses and in shopping malls. Like a walking stick, (rather than a cane, which suggests infirmity), the umbrella extends the arm and thus the personal space of the holder, which can have a megalomaniac effect on fragile souls.

Academy Duello, Vancouver's only duelling club, teaches courses in the use of the umbrella for self-defence. But even if it is only the power to dispense the temporary shelter once reserved for nobles, as the Hollies song suggests, being able to take a friend "under your roof," out of the rain, still implies a degree of primal yet gentlemanly *machismo*.

The first niche-market exclusive umbrella shop in the world, James Smith and Sons, at 53 New Oxford Street, London, opened in 1830 and still purveys portable shelter to discriminating strollers. In 1852, the brolly joined the Industrial Revolution when Samuel Fox invented a steel rib design using lighter fabrics, which quickly supplanted the heavy constructions of wood, whalebone and alpaca or oiled canvas that previously prevented a soaking.

To make them more fashionable when furled, umbrellas adopted the now traditional hook handle borrowed from walking canes, a shortened shepherds' crook. Craftsmen trained to turn hard woods like ebony and malacca, favoured for walking sticks and umbrella handles, commanded high dough. Doctors, who made house calls at all hours in any weather, were among the first to popularize the umbrella, just as they adopted the caped Inverness overcoat. Sensible chaps. Unlike the high school boys of my generation, who could never have picked up a chick using that "Please share my umbrella" line. Despite the appalling chemical interaction of rain and Bryclreem, the moment it stopped raining proverbial canines and felines, we "lost" our umbrellas on the first available bus or in some coffee shop booth. Our mothers were spared financial ruin by the fact that these umbrellas were bought on sale at Eaton's or The Bay for around ten dollars. Like gumboots and early model Fords, they came in any colour you wanted as long as it was black and they had a chromed tip the nastier little bastards among us would file to a point.

## Beats Shovellin' It

You can still buy umbrellas for around the same price. They come in colours now, but the handles are still made of what seems to be pressed sawdust with a 'genuine wood-grain finish.' The cheapest sources of portable shelter are actually the coat-check rooms of nightclubs, cafes and restaurants, which always have a ready supply of forgotten and unclaimed umbrellas

Brollies of quality will naturally have been dibbed by discriminating underpaid staff, but if you have to step out into an unexpectedly dark and stormy night, it's worth demonstrating to the doorperson, host or hostess that you may be forced to shelter under a tiny $10 bill. Most of them will be happy to trade you for a bumbershoot that cost them zip. Unfashionable, only partly functional, it will get you and a friend to the car, cab, or bus stop with a suave display of personal resourcefulness. It may even become a funny souvenir of the beginning of a romance.

If you must fuss about what you use to keep the rain off, there are umbrellas that make serious fashion and cultural statements; brollies decorated with reproductions of the Sistine Chapel ceiling or prints of French Impressionists, especially Georges Seurat, in whose painting *Dimanche a Grande Jatte* parasols are a recurring motif. Prince Rupert may be the true rain capital of the West coast, but Vancouver supported its own umbrella boutique and factory, The Umbrella Shop at 534 W. Pender, for sixty years.

If you must invest in an umbrella that parades your good taste and possession of more dollars than sense, don't be suckered by designer names. Open it and check the ribs. If they're hollow fluted tubes, you're buying a label that may not provide much shelter from the storm. In a quality umbrella, ribs should be made of solid steel, more resistant to wind and rough handling, which also makes it a more useful item of self-defence, as some of us learned in high school. Still, it's silly to over-pay for an item that will make you feel like you flushed your Rolex down the toilet when you lose it. Because you *will* lose it—on a bus, in a cab, in a restaurant, night club, or in a coffee shop with a condensation-steamed window where some genius at the counter inevitably observes, "Beats shovellin' it."

One thing you can take to the bank: after two days of nail-driving rain, the clouds will lift and the sun will shine. Here on the Wet Coast, we call it "Monday."

SEVEN

# Prozac.calm

No group of professionals likes to have its competence questioned by non-professionals and all professionals regard the phrase *professional journalist* as an oxymoron. When this article was published in the Vancouver Sun, I expected a stake and kindling; at least a public flaying in Letters to the Editor. Instead, I got a flattering letter from the head of the Department of Psychiatry at the University of British Columbia. Go figure.

Cruising the banner-plastered cyber-lanes of the Information Highway late one night, depressed by weeks of Vancouver's low clouds and rain, exhausted by insomnia, I pulled into a commercial rest area, www.prozac.com, to cool my search engine and check the mileage on my psychodometer. On the misery-loves-company premise, I'd already made a pit-stop at www.statscan.ca and clicked on the mental health numbers to see how many of my fellow Canadians were as bummed out as I was. According to the latest data, I was one of 1,314,000, though most of us would cheer up in two to four weeks. Average number of weeks depressed, however, is double that: 7.5 weeks. Almost two months! A small percentage of chronically depressed people are obviously carrying more than their fair share of the unbearable weight of being.

Most of them are women. In every age bracket, the number of depressed women is almost double that of blue men. Check out the high-risk, mid-life (age 35-44) group: 834,000 women to 480,000 men. The baseline age of the table is twelve. If that seems shockingly young, reference tables on suicide for the teenage range. I'd been shocked by encounters with teens and early twenties, girls who blithely admitted to taking prescribed anti-depressants, some since puberty. A recent article in the *Vancouver Sun* noted that anti-depressants like Serax, Prozac and Valium are still the drugs most commonly prescribed for women.

In public, I'm Dean Martin, highball in hand, slurring "I hate to advocate drugs and alcohol but they've always worked for me," yet I watched helplessly as a beautiful older female friend destroyed herself with gin and tranquillizers. I was too ashamed to attend her funeral because I hadn't done anything to stop her slow-motion suicide. I had no idea *what* to do. She was a grown woman, independently wealthy and, I suspect, literally bored to death by her life.

As for www.prozac.com, several of my female friends going through rocky divorces were taking prescribed Prozac, so I checked out the site. Email aside, the internet has proved a bit of a bust where genuine communication is concerned, except for the marginal loners whose participation in chat rooms of an astonishing variety of weirdness at least gives them the illusion of having a life. Most of the Net has already been colonized by advertising. Every company on the planet seems to have a self-promoting website and major pharmaceutical companies are no exception. Some of their potential customers are those people most likely to be surfing the ether in the middle of the night, researching the sources of their insomnia and unhappiness.

At www.prozac.com, soothing and cheerful pale yellow backgrounds with navigation borders of reassuringly cool dark blue guide the visitor to Disease Information, Caring for Others, Community Support (a virtual group-therapy chat room) but always inevitably back to *fluoxetine hydrochloride*, a.k.a. Prozac. I discovered that 18 million Americans suffer from some form of depression, while only one million currently take Prozac to combat clinical depression, bulimia and other related obsessive-compulsive disorders.

The implication is that 17 million depressed people have yet to see the light—shame, shame. Judging by the number of downbeat, overweight, underweight, obsessive nut-cases you meet on an average road trip south of the 49th parallel—say on a four-day Las Vegas junket—American cities might consider the viability of injecting bulk *fluoxetine hydrochloride* directly into their municipal water systems instead of dealing with the problem on a labour-intensive case-by-case basis.

Some html whiz-kid could jazz up the Prozac main page by adding graphics of a guy pondering a .38 calibre nightcap, a bulimic disgorging an entire Sara Lee pound cake into a toilet, an OCD sufferer compulsively scrubbing bleeding chapped hands, but that would be in questionable taste. Porn websites carry teasers showing people doing things you might not dream of doing in the privacy of your own bedroom, but mental illness is a subject about which humour has become unforgivable. Witness the shit-storms in a pill bottle that erupted over movies like *What About Bob?* and *Me, Myself and Irene*.

## The Irish Psychiatrist

If you're snickering, you're laughing at me, not with me. I was treated for severe depression thirty years ago. Despite a failed marriage and an aborted career, I wasn't indulging in the mawkish they'll-be-sorry-when-I'm-gone fantasies of the self-pitying shmeeb. I was merely having difficulty making qualitative existential distinctions between actions. For example, standing on a corner I couldn't decide whether 'twas nobler in the mind to step into a cafe for coffee or to step out in front of a hurtling Broadway bus. There didn't seem to be a difference I could make an argument for. I was concerned that I might end up like one of those scientists who tests a hypothesis on himself and whose last words are "Oh, shit..."

Before Prozac got the U.S. FDA seal of approval in 1987, a popular treatment for this risky ambivalence was Serax, the little yellow pill the Rolling Stones sang about in "Mother's Little Helper." I took Serax under the supervision of a psychiatrist, as Prozac recommends for its product. I never caught a bus the hard way, so maybe it worked. My psychiatrist was an atypical Irishman—neither talkative nor charming—but he helped me get back the sense of humour I'd mislaid in Hell's waiting room. I invented a character I call The Irish Psychiatrist, who listens to your whining rationalizations for an hour in unresponsive silence, then says, "Well, Ay see are tayme's up for t'dye. Go 'round t' Father O'Blivion and make a true confession of yer sins. Come round t' the pub after for a quayet jar."

Our relationship ended over the magazines in his waiting room. As other patients exited, snivelling from cathartic revelations I envied, I read articles in *Time* and *Newsweek* about women in El Salvador and Nicaragua going into cornfields of a morning to try to identify the headless, handless corpses of husbands, brothers, and sons murdered and mutilated by right-wing death squads. I voiced the suggestion that my stress might be small beer and asked the Irish Psychiatrist if his skills as an MD and mental health professional might not be better employed treating survivors of such atrocities. The Doctor became defensive and hostile. I diagnosed a guilt complex and incipient paranoia and replaced him with Dr. John Jameson, a double shot of which my bartender dispenses whenever I say, "I'd like to see the Irish Psychiatrist, please."

## Better Living through Chemistry

Resisting the croaking of friends who resolved mental crises by becoming born-again Christians, Scientologists or chanting Buddhists, I continued taking anti-depressants for a while on a scrip from my GP, the late and deeply missed Dr. George Chalmers. George was one of those old-school family doctors who not only listened; he talked back, offering candid advice based on his own life experiences as well as his medical expertise. He often did more good in a forty-minute chat across his desk than most psychiatrists do in months of hourly sessions. I didn't appreciate that until I'd wasted months on the metaphorical couch of the Irish Psychiatrist.

I also took Halcion, a mild hypnotic for the insomnia I've endured since my teens. Later research indicated that prolonged Halcion use induces psychotic hallucinations, but in the short time I used it, both it and Serax did what psychoactive drugs are supposed to do. "I'm not a mechanic. My job isn't to adjust you to the status quo," my shrink told me while he and the pharmaceutical industry did their damnedest to do exactly that. Prozac admits it's no cure for depression. It merely enables victims of what its makers claim is a chemical imbalance in the brain to get to work by catching a bus in the socially approved manner.

With the mapping of 97% of the human genome and the development of drugs like Prozac, we're within a swallow of becoming the engineered humans—dutifully taking their Soma to ensure emotional calm—predicted by Aldous Huxley in his visionary 1932 novel, *Brave New World*. In his 1950s essays, *The Doors of Perception*, Huxley again raised the question of whether pharmaceutically-induced tranquillity is preferable to unpleasant but authentic mental states. He noted the North American tendency to outlaw psychotropic drugs that stimulate the mind (LSD, mescaline, cannabis sativa) while endorsing drugs that suppress anti-social behaviour by mere stupefaction—Thorazine and its secular cousins, widely advertised in the pages of glossy magazines.

Anyone who has known someone afflicted with schizophrenia appreciates the good psychoactive drugs can do. But true schizophrenia is a grab bag of psychotic symptoms that afflicts only about one percent of populations worldwide, with a higher incidence in industrially developed nations.

If more than 18 million Americans already suffer from depression—probably a conservative estimate that doesn't take into account the millions more who misuse alcohol to self-medicate depression under the guise of partying—it suggests that using any chemical substance to suppress symptoms of this widespread social disease is like applying Bactine and a Pooh Bear Band-Aid to a gangrenous gunshot wound.

## Just Say Yes to Drugs

"You can get into a hell of a fugue on Serax and beer," a woman warned me at a party in a second-floor walk-up on Commercial Drive. "I can get into a hell of a fugue without either of them," I replied, tossing the blister pack of Serax at my unfinished brew as I groped through the cloud of second-hand Ganja to the door.

More than four decades of research have led me to conclude that depression is the sane and sober response to the conditions of contemporary urban life. I now regard my relapses as episodes of painful but precious lucidity. In the 19th century, they called it melancholia, a condition that has affected many poets, artists, and musicians since the Romantic Movement. In post-slavery African-American culture, it's called the blues, the most potent seminal music style of the 20th century. Would any doctor seriously put someone like T-Bone Walker on Prozac to stop him singing, "They call it stormy Monday, but Tuesday's just as bad?" Would it be better to turn him into a Sammy Davis Jr., grinning out "The Candyman Can" to an audience of bulimic white folks bulked up on all-you-can-eat buffet prime rib, free scotch, and prescription anti-depressants?

"Depression is not a character flaw. It is not a 'mood' or a personality weakness you can change at will or by 'pulling yourself together'," counsels www.prozac.com, offering an it's-not-your-fault virtual hug that reinforces the "just say yes to drugs" message. This is where advertising shifts from buffing the truth in the interests of marketing to barefaced bull-shitting in the grand tradition of snake oil peddlers of the storied past.

There *are* things you can do. Exercise, even pointless laps around a track or pumping weights, is therapeutic. Hiking and rock-climbing, both recommended by Huxley in his flawed didactic final novel, *Island*, are rewarding on more levels. Mastering any physical activity you've been shy of, from cunnilingus to karate, works like an amphetamine enema, producing an endorphin-jacked sense of empowerment and reconnection to the world that demands a triumphant ice-cold beer instead of a slug of tepid water to wash down a pill. If you're not ready for kickboxing classes, get a book or video on yoga and do it for twenty minutes every day in the privacy of your squalid illegal basement suite. It'll loosen your chakras whether you believe in it or not.

D oing what you really *want* to do is the best therapy. Instead of fighting it, I've learned to appreciate my chronic insomnia for creating quiet time to write in. Above my desk, an old *New Yorker* cartoon shows a landscaping guy leaning on a rake, telling a co-worker, "I used to be a famous novelist until I was cured of alcoholism and depression and my work went all to hell." Even surfing the Net to sites like www.prozac.com or www.feelingblue.com, run by the Glaxo Smith Kline drug titan, can make you feel better.

I took the free Zung Depression Self-Assessment Test on offer and scored 36.25. A score of 50 indicates you should take a print-off to your doctor. Rack 75 or 80, you should be speed-dialling a Suicide Prevention Hotline or 911. Every page of www.prozac.com offers a push-button to "email this page to a friend," so I forwarded them all to my editors at the *Vancouver Sun*.

Double-checking the symptoms list, I got to "loss of interest in sex," hit File/Close/Shutdown and segued to the master bedroom for a bit of Australian Foreplay—the old nudge and whisper, "You awake?" Got an elbow in the eye and dozed off humming the crucifixion musical number from Monty Python's *The Life of Brian*, "Always look on the bright side of life..." Woke up to Cheerios with the kids, stacked John Lee Hooker CDs on shuffle-play, boogied in my underwear with my baby daughter in my arms in front of the open living room curtains, laughing at the rain, and scared the crap out of the neighbours, who already think I'm deranged.

Okay, maybe I am crazy. It's nothing to be depressed about.

EIGHT

# Finding My Marbles

I still have my marbles. A few, at least. Found with other things I haven't known what to do with, except to put in a safe place—my wife's dry euphemism for *lost*. At the bottom of a softening liquor box with a collection of obscene Javanese kris handles, a globe of the moon, a manuscript of short stories I'd forgotten I'd written, envelopes stuffed with letters from mislaid friends, I found a handful of small cat's-eyes. I grabbed them like a salvage diver snatching jewels and doubloons from the sandy sea-bottom grave of a sunken galleon.

Rolling them in my palm, I savoured the sibilant clicking and practised my impression of Bogart doing Captain Queeg's courtroom mad scene from *The Caine Mutiny*. The sensation in my fingers took me back to childhood schoolyards, recesses and lunch hours exhausted in the massed charges and masked brutalities of British Bulldog, or with girls who showed their underpants and sometimes more behind green painted wooden backstops we flicked our baseball cards against, one landing nearest the wall winning, and—inevitably—to marble season.

At my own kids' elementary school some years ago, I overheard the Principal making the PA announcement officially banning all *Pokemon, Digimon,* and *Yu-Gi-Oh* trading cards because students had been bullying each other to acquire them. In Quebec, a boy had been stabbed in the schoolyard in an anime trading card deal that went bad. Despite clever multimedia marketing of the cartoon versions of Pokemon and a hydra of spin-offs, *Digimon, Dragonball Z, Yu-Gi-Oh* and *BeyBlades* as video games, toys, and trading cards, the whole shelf of "pocket monsters" seemed to be on a crash trajectory for the same seldom-opened junk drawer, attic or crawlspace box where once-treasured baseball and hockey cards and bags of chipped and worn marbles repose like the funeral goods of a young Pharaoh.

What kids remember where they left the obsessive fads of the last two decades—the Pogs or Kinder Surprise toys, the Tamigotchi Eggs and the whole brood of "electronic pets" they spawned? How quickly they became just little bits of unidentifiable plastic on the floor for parents to step on in the dark and toss in the trash with a muted curse. With no marketing whatever, marble season returned every year to elementary school playgrounds when I was a kid.

No overt attempt was made to control or curtail marble season, but no one ever got stabbed over marbles either. In the 1950s, marbles were still seen by the adult world as a quaint detail from a Norman Rockwell illustration, the harmless pastime of boys in knickerbockers; a relic of a simpler time. School officials sensed marble season was an infinitely more complex social phenomenon than it appeared, but they couldn't penetrate its mysteries any more than an undergraduate anthropologist could wrangle an invitation to a genuine voodoo ceremony. In fact, marbles were the currency of an underground economy, as arbitrary, exclusive, secret, and ruthless as any black market.

## The Alley Mercantile

Marble season arrived like a recurrent plague, a kind of brain fever afflicting male children only. Girls "skipped," using single and double ropes, or long strings of knotted coloured elastics attached to a fixed stanchion at one end and wrapped around a girl's leg at the other—called Chinese Skip—to create complex choreographies accompanied by song-chants, some of very ancient origin, which still haunt my dreams of childhood. Marbles was a boys' game.

There were no warning symptoms of the onset of its season. Large numbers of boys would just turn up at school one day with marbles rattling in their pockets and Lone Ranger lunch kits. Within days, marble bags swung from every wrist. Smaller than a gym-strip bag, these were often likewise sewn by mothers from scraps of fabric leftover from McCalls dress patterns that had come to grief on the rocks of busy motherhood. The primo marble bag was the purple velvet bag with the golden cord that proclaimed parents with the taste and income to drink Seagram's Crown Royal Canadian whisky.

That purple bag was as much a status symbol as the number and quality of its contents. But, like a gem dealer's inventory, the marbles it held weren't just "marbles." There was a ranking system of value as arcane as any you'd find behind the steel doors of the Diamond Club in New York or Amsterdam. That I still recall it in detail testifies to its power over boys of my age.

Most common were cat's-eyes: small clear glass spheres with

wafers of colour suspended inside like a child's hand windmill. Rarer were the ones we called dates; opaque white marbles the same size as cat's-eyes, but with streaks and swirls of yellow, black and brown sweeping across their surfaces like storms on Jupiter. I always secretly liked dates because they suggested mysterious planets or exotic candies. Despite their rarity, in the official ranking they were worth less than cat's-eyes and the rule of the marble market was more absolute than the loop-holed regulations of any Securities and Exchange Commission. If you walked onto the school grounds with a bag full of dates you'd be laughed off the yard, so I kept mine in a drawer at home, a private vice, along with my collection of matchbook covers from exotic motels and illustrated trout flies torn from the backs of discarded Sportsman cigarette packs I risked hepatitis to fish out of ditches.

Higher in value than cat's-eyes, which we called alleys generically, were crystals. The same size as regular alleys, crystals had no internal leaves of colour, but weren't clear. A suggestive cosmic drift of tiny bubbles and a subtle colour tint distinguished them. Like tiny self-contained galaxies, they were hypnotically beautiful, instantly collectible and worth a heaping handful of cat's-eyes.

Above them were cobs—three times the size of the average cat's-eye. Though most contained the same internal colour-wafer structure, they were worth a dozen or more regular marbles in a straight trade. More rare and valuable still were crystal cobs. Nearer the apex of value were king cobs—giant marbles, double the size of a cob but still cat's-eyes.

At the top of the market, the ultimate prize of every marble collector, as unique and covetable as the Hope Diamond or Star of India, was the Crystal King Cob. This was a marble you paid in alleys just to *see* briefly, to touch only if the owner was a best friend or someone who owed you for the loan of a rare comic book. They were almost never traded. To possess one was to be famous and revered.

Steelies occupied a special category. Nothing more than ball bearings of various sizes, the legitimacy of steelies as marbles was always in dispute. Most kids refused to shoot against steelies with glass marbles because of the extra punch they packed and the devaluing chipping they caused.

## Childhood's Casino

Like trading cards, marbles could be used to play games, but in their purest sense they constituted an economy in themselves. Arbitrary tokens of value—money by another name—they temporarily possessed what anthropologists call *mana*: power or virtue. They were the chips of childhood's casino. Only geeky kids *played* with them. I remember only two games they were used in— the traditional thumb-shot into a circle in the dirt, a miniature version of the ancient game of bowls, and Chase, a pointless excuse for kids with only a few marbles to wander the margins of the playground, pretending to have something to do by flicking marbles in a hare-and-hounds ground level game of tag.

The real action in marble season was in the covered playground, where the marble kings set up their pitches like carny gypsies. This was the marble midway, trading floor of the Alley Mercantile Exchange, the recess bazaar, the pre-teen souk, where young hustlers set up shop with no more than a precious marble and a line in the dirt. Scoring a shooting fault-line with a Keds sneaker heel, they would pace off the distance and sit, legs apart, with the prize presented between their spread knees.

The proposition was simple: shoot from behind the line, hit

the offered marble and it was yours. Misses rolled into the crotch of dusty jeans and were swiftly swept into the marble-bag of the operator. An operator might lose two Cobs, but gain dozens of alleys he could trade for three or four more Cobs with neighbouring entrepreneurs. Soprano pitchmen hawked their wares:"Cawb here!" or "Crysssss-tal Cob!" "King Cob hee-ah!"

It was a cacophonous casbah in which neophytes were frequently fleeced, their marble-bags left as flaccid as a eunuch's scrotum by sharp dealing. A thumb-snapped sphere of glass moves fast and takes unpredictable hops on a sneaker-scrubbed pitch. The unwritten rule was that the struck marble had to move. One of the lower tricks of the trade was to knuckle the offered prize into the dirt, like a golf ball in a soft sand trap, and deny even clear hits on the grounds that the big cob on offer hadn't moved. An obvious dodge was to present a big cob steelie, but no one but a total dinkweed would shoot at that.

Some kids take to dealing instinctively. Their marble bags always bulged and even when they seemed to lose, they recouped their glass fortunes quickly, like eccentric tycoons. Marbles taught them more than the arts of acquisition. The fundamental dichotomy of being a marble king became clear when they realized that marbles in themselves didn't constitute real wealth. Marbles couldn't be converted into coin for Mars bars, *Hot Rod* magazines or cigarettes you swore you were buying for your Mom and later shared in the ravines behind the school. Their value existed only within the closed system of marble season economics.

## Scramble

To fully enjoy the status conferred by packing a big bag, alley tycoons had to prolong marble season for as long as possible, even though their own gifts for sharp trading and acquisition worked against that end. If the bulk of the theoretical wealth in the system became concentrated too quickly in too few hands, losing kids would lose interest in marbles and their parents would stop buying replacements at the Totem Five & Dime. The problem of re-distribution of wealth in a closed system was solved in a manner reminiscent of the once-banned potlatch ceremonies of First Nations people of the Pacific Northwest.

Having amassed a glass fortune by skill and guile, the marble millionaire could only achieve legendary status by a gesture so grandiose, so contrary to market principles, it was absurdly heroic. He'd hold a big scramble. Small scrambles were a frequent source of impromptu entertainment. Marble kings routinely amused themselves by pulling a valuable marble from their bags without warning, tossing it into the air and shouting, "Scramble on a crystal!" or "Scramble on a cob!", just for the pleasure of watching lesser mortals grovel and grapple in the gravel over the unexpected prize. But this was small change, like a dot-com tycoon tipping a waiter a C-note for serving dessert after hours.

The big scramble was not a spontaneous gesture. It was a sacred ritual planned for a specific time—not after school was out at 3 p.m., because witnesses would disperse homeward too quickly, dissipating the adulation. Scrambles were held at lunch hour, so morning recess could be spent passing the word to create anticipation and suspense. For the rest of the morning, the announced host would then be treated with the exaggerated deference paid in some cultures to human sacrifices before their immolation.

At the lunch bell, the ritual host-victim would retire to the boys washroom with his most trusted attendants to prepare himself and allow twenty minutes or so for starving kids to gobble their tuna or bologna sandwiches and gather below the appointed high place—a large rock, stump or concrete Exit ramp. Lugging a bag bulging at the seams with precious alleys, the anointed one would at last appear and mount the altar to the respectful murmur of the crowd and the rustle of crumpled lunch bags. Surveying the reverent congregation below, he would savour the moment, then hold the great bag aloft and shout as loud as a boy's unbroken voice would allow, the sacred incantation: "Scraaaaambull!"

Opening the neck of the bag, he would swing it by a bottom corner in a violent, almost sexual, transport of ecstasy, creating spiral nebulae of shining gem-like interruptions of the atmosphere that arced and fell to earth like tracer bullets or errant meteors, wounding the spectators, who convulsed like a single captive Caliban under the glittering lash. Alone in triumph, he savoured the spectacle of earthly power as the marble-maddened mob grubbed in the mud, snatched, slapped, punched, kicked, bit, and tore from each others' hands, pockets, and bags.

Without a single marble in his orgasm-drained bag, the erstwhile marble king would descend and walk among the grovelling *hoi polloi*—apart, aloof, a kind of playground God for a day; holy, untouchable. Next morning at recess, he'd set up his pitch with a few hoarded cobs and start all over again.

## The Rich Are Different

Teachers were sensibly suspicious of marble season. They saw the accurate if superficial parallel between marbles and the ring-toss hustles of the carnival midway. But they still thought of marbles as toys, like the big teddy bears or trashy souvenir prizes that were all you could win at Playland. Because they never saw marbles as wealth, they never understood that marbles constituted a microeconomy, a network of mergers and acquisitions, hostile takeovers, investment and return and, above all, risk.

Gambling is almost universal in human societies, no matter how primitive, including the larval societies of childhood. The universal appeal of gambling lies not in the possibility of gain, but in the possibility of change, of altering the existing social order. Win the 649 Lottery or go to Vegas, bet the farm on ten the hard way and roll double fives, draw to an inside straight at the big money table or tickle that SuperJackpot pokie machine and you're suddenly rich. And, as F. Scott Fitzgerald observed to Ernest Hemingway, "The rich are different."

Despite Hem's deflationary reply, "Yes, they have more money," Fitz was right, if not exactly in the way he meant. To those who inherit or acquire great wealth, gambling affords merely the lame *frisson* that accompanies losing more money in a few minutes than most people will ever possess without suffering unduly. As organized crime and national, state, and provincial governments know too well, the real gamblers are the poor, for whom the prize is nothing less than the transformation of life. That's what marble season offered: an opportunity for hustle to triumph over muscle, for skill and brains to beat the customary brawn-and-bluster status quo of the schoolyard.

A bully might acquire marbles quickly by intimidation, but he'd lose them as fast to someone half his size at one of the shooting galleries and everyone would know how he came by them anyway and hold him in utter contempt. Bullies who'd pride themselves on extorting lunch money wouldn't dare hijack a fat marble-bag because when word got around, they'd actually *lose* status for breaking the house rules of childhood's casino. Like being banned from the only bar in a small northern town if you're a bad drunk, the old Native tribal system of being "cast out" for certain transgressions still works.

Marble season literally levelled the playing field with sneaker heels. It squared a lot of social scores that would otherwise have been settled more predictably and bloodily at the yellow bridge after school. It gave mere bullies pause and let some unlikely heroes take a brief glorious walk in the sun. Marble season taught us more about the nature of value, market economies, social status, and real life than anything we learned in twelve years of school.

In one of the Dollar Stores that are inflation's answer to the old Five & Dime as a kid's Cave of the Forty Thieves, I re-discovered marbles I hadn't seen in forty years. A cob, a handful of cat's-eyes, even a few dates, nestled in little net bags I hefted in the palms of my hands. For the price of the one and two dollar coins destroying the pocket lining of my slacks almost as fast as the government is devaluing our currency, I could become the marble king I always dreamed of being.

That would be cheating, so I only bought one bag, just to keep the old ones company in the rotting box at home. They don't have marble season at my kids' school. Even anime trading cards are passé. The phone app and video-game wired generation don't seem to collect anything specific at the moment, but they will. Marble season taught us that it's human nature to invest trivial objects with abstract value, whether they're cowrie shells, crystal cobs, Bitcoins, bills, certificates of deposit, or corporations.

Money is an abstraction, a symbol, a physical token, that supposedly represents the value of goods or human labour. Some of us learned to simply substitute money for marbles (marbles=money) and keep playing the game as if the one with the biggest Crown

Royal bag wins, becoming *entrepreneurs* in the 1980s, when being called one in print was reason to break out the Cristal Brut. Others interpreted the same lesson with the opposite conclusion, seeing that money=marbles is not the same thing at all.

I'm hanging on to my marbles and trolling flea markets for a faded velvet Crown Royal bag to keep them in. When all the Pokemon cards, Game Boys, electronic pets, gaming systems, and phone apps finally end up in the landfill with all the dreck of the last half-century, I'm going to teach my kids how to scuff out a pitch on top of the bulldozed grave mound of western civilization and yell, "King cob heeee-ah!" in a voice that'll have a new generation lining up to lose their marbles.

NINE

# Sukiyaki

Kyu who?

I'm haunted by Kyu Sakamoto. When his big hit, "Sukiyaki," was re-reborn on the radio ethernet, harmonized in English by a slick R&B quartet calling themselves 4 P.M. (For Postive Music), the uniquely evocative melody was almost as big a hit as it had been when Kyu's Japanese original dominated the AM airwaves more than thirty years before.

"Kyu who?" was the response I got from anyone under the age of forty-five when I remarked it was nice to see a cover of such a great oldie enjoy such a renaissance. More than a few, especially young women obviously under the spell of 4 P.M.'s male-model charm and syrupy vocalizing, looked at me like I was just another old man who'd mixed up his medications.

"Like, you're saying, like, some random guy actually had, like, a number one hit *way* back in 1963 singing this song...in, like, *Japanese?*"

My wife was one of them. She was born in 1963. When I thought about it, it did sound seriously weird. Lucky for me, Rhino Records has made a business of re-issuing compilations of *Billboard* magazine's top pop hits that preserve the actual sounds of the times.

Though it's been decades since I've heard the original played on one of the many "classic rock" radio stations still making a buck by patronizing the big demographic boomers, Rhino's 1963 compilation (Catalogue no.17584) bears me out. A glance at the rest of the track list on the CD is like viewing an epileptic's encephalograph.

## You Had to Be There

I was undergoing the trauma of male puberty at the time—an event that, for me at least, overshadowed the Cuban Missile Crisis, which turned out to be a sort of coming attractions trailer for nuclear Armageddon that fortunately flopped at the box office. Like Cold War politics, pop music was in an uncertain holding pattern. Nobody in un-amplified distance of Greenwich Village had heard of Bob Dylan, but he was at least working a popular genre. Folkies held *hootenannies*—sort of like raves, only with candles in raffia-wrapped chianti bottles instead of a laser light shows and caffeine instead of Ecstasy—and no, they weren't as much fun. Mainstream folk chart-toppers that year included the bouncy "Walk Right In" by The Rooftop Singers and the darker oddity, "Sally Go Round the Roses" by The Jaynetts.

Tin Pan Alley cats still prowled the Brill Building, producing such classic teen tear-jerkers as The Cascades' "Rhythm of the Rain" complete with storm sound effects, but they were losing their edge in dreck like "Hey Paula" by the gag-cutesy duet, Paul & Paula. Bobby Vinton, one of many Brylcreemed Bobbies destined to be preserved for posterity in the neon tar-pits of Las Vegas lounges, (Bobby Vee, Bobby Rydell, Bobby Darin, Bobby Curtola), crooned "Blue Velvet" that year, a schlock ballad that would become the ironic theme and title of David Lynch's savage, surreal, sexually explicit postmodern nouveau film noir three decades later.

Surf music by instrumental reverb guitar combos like The Ventures, building on edgier work by legendary guitarists Dick Dale, Link Wray and Duane Eddy, was still huge. Two classics of the genre made the charts that year: "Pipeline" by The Chantays and "Wipe Out" by The Surfaris. But strangely, 1963 also produced two top hits sung in foreign languages: "Dominque," an irritating repetitive folkie curio by a guitar-strumming Singing Nun, and "Sukiyaki," a haunting incomprehensible ballad by Kyu Sakamoto. Neither Kyu nor the Singing Nun ever had another North American hit, but for a year you couldn't get within earshot of a transistor radio for long enough to smoke a cigarette swiped from your Mom's pack without hearing them.

## It's Not Your Party, Lesley, Go Cry Somewhere Else

On June 15, 1963, Kyu Sakamoto's peculiarly named song bumped Lesley Gore's teen-whiner, "It's My Party (And I'll Cry If I Want To)," off the top step to become the Number One pop song in the U.S. Even Rhino turns up its snout at Gore's juvenile slop, failing to include it in the compilation. A sort of female Bobby with varnished bee-hive hair, sheath dress and sling-back heels, Gore must've asked herself, "Kyu who?" and "What the hell is Sukiyaki?"

She didn't run out and enrol in Japanese classes at night school, or French either. Like "Dominque," "Sukiyaki" had 'novelty hit' written all over it and Gore had a string of Tin Pan Alley charters that all involved somebody crying because somebody else was wearing some Bobby or Johnny's class ring or varsity sweater. Her songs were the hormonal soundtrack for the Archie and Veronica comic scenarios acted out in our high school halls. They didn't know it, but Gore and other girl singers like Connie-Where the

Boys Are-Francis were already on their way out of town without so much as a bus ticket to Reno.

What was sukiyaki? Who was Kyu? Nobody knew. Most deejays never really said. They just played the thing until the grooves wore out. I remember one, no doubt Red Robinson, since he was the best-informed deejay on the Vancouver airwaves at the time, explaining that the song was about a guy who'd lost his true love. What makes the song's popularity such an amazing phenomenon is that everybody in North America knew that *already* even though the only word of Japanese most of them knew was *sayonara*.

Which raises an interesting question—why wasn't the song called *Sayonara*? It means 'farewell' in Japanese. Given the song's theme, it would've made a lot more sense. Why *Sukiyaki*?

## Excuse Please, This Fish Is Underdone

To bolster my I-told-you-so aura of omniscience among the young, I consulted the postmodern oracle, the Internet. A search for 'sukiyaki' turned up enough recipes to qualify me as a short order cook in some undiscriminating backwoods prefecture of the Land of The Rising Sun and a couple of porn sites devoted to fetishes so specialized they only have intimidating Japanese names I'm afraid to investigate for fear of giving my email address to the *yakuza*, not to mention finding out things about myself I don't want to know. But I finally got the true *gen* on sukiyaki and Kyu Sakamoto.

For the record, sukiyaki is a Japanese rustic stew based on a broth of sake and soy sauce, containing vegetables, tofu and meat, a warming dish of welcome for guests or a family one-pot meal. During the long Edo Period (1600-1868), eating beef was prohibited on Buddhist principles. Cattle were few and their by-products precious. The prohibition was lifted during the Meiji Period (1868-1912), the era when Japan finally opened its doors and began aping Western manners and technology.

Why was the name of a stew hung on Kyu's big international hit? Because in 1963 sukiyaki was one of the few Japanese words North Americans recognized and the only Japanese dish anyone ate. I know life before sushi is hard to imagine, but neither it nor sashimi were in the cultural vocabulary. If some hakimachi-ed chef handed you a wad of sticky rice and seaweed wrapped around a slice of raw tuna topped with fish roe and a cracked quail's egg, you'd have horked all over the bar long before George Bush Sr. made projectile vomiting an instrument of international diplomacy.

### The Japanese Bobby Darin

Check out www.japanorama.com/kyuchan.html if you want this from the other end of the horse. According to this Kyu-worship site, "The explanation is simple: intercultural ignorance. Western DJs needed a song title that was at once easily pronounceable and associated with Japan. So Sukiyaki was it, even though the word is not mentioned in the song."

Affectionately named Kyu-chan, Sakamoto Kyu, to be correctly Japanese, was born in Kawasaki, Kanagawa Prefecture, in 1941. He made his show business debut at nineteen in 1960, topping the Nippon charts with a monster hit "Ue o Muite Aruko (I Look Up When I Walk)," which would become "Sukiyaki" two years later when it was released in the west. Pictures show a handsome young man with greased back hair, in a tux, looking every inch the junior Rat-Packer, a Japanese Bobby Darin or Paul Anka.

Beloved in Japan for his sincerity and charming smile as well as his captivating voice, he had other hits we never heard, "Shiawase Nara Te o Tatako" and "Miagete Goran Sora no Hoshi o," but one young man I ranted at about Kyu during a replay of the 4 P.M. version mentioned him to a group of young Japanese skiers at Whistler afterwards and was overwhelmed by their response.

"It was like I'd asked them about Elvis," he admitted. I permitted him to grovel before my vindicated and vastly superior wisdom without putting the boot in too hard.

Like Elvis, Kyu has left the building. On August 12, 1985, he was a passenger on JAL flight 123, a Boeing 747 that lost pieces of its tail section after taking off from Haneda airport. The plane spiralled downward for thirty minutes, long enough for most of the 520 passengers aboard to scribble farewells to their families that were later found among the wreckage on a mountain sixty miles north of Tokyo. It was one of the worst, and certainly the most poignant, air disasters in history.

## The Song Remains the Same—Comparative Lyric 100

Credit for the initial success of "Sukiyaki" and its endurance must go to composers Hachidai Nakamura and Rokusuke Ei. Like Kyu, they had absorbed Japan's post-occupation ethic of imitating all things American thoroughly. Behind its nominally oriental sound-gloss, Nakamura's music is straight from the Tin Pan Alley ashcan; verse, chorus, bridge, verse, chorus, which in large part explains why almost any free transliteration of the lyrics works so well.

Rokusuke Ei's original lyrics are said to have been inspired by his despair at being rejected in love by the Japanese actress, Meiko Nakamura, no relation to his collaborator. The website publishes the lyrics in Romanized phonetic Japanese, in case you want to really blow away a karaoke bar some night, as well as in an English transliteration, an approximation of the heavily inflected, imagistic Japanese original.

The dominant image is the now mildewed equation of rain/tears.

The opening line, also the original title, translates as "I look up when I walk/ so the tears won't fall." In a neat bit of cross-cultural synchronicity, the song's theme and imagery are almost identical to that of The Cascades "Rhythm of the Rain" released the same year with actual rain sound-effects, though no one but an eccentric Japanese scholar would've picked up that connection at the time.

4 P.M.'s 1994 transliteration is admirably faithful to the original, employing the same motif of looking up at the sky and treating it as an emotional weather-report: "You went away/ Now my life is just a rainy day" and "If you were only here/ you'd wash away my tears/ The sun would shine/ Once again you'd be mine all mine," reinforcing the repeated rejected lover's refrain, "You took your love away from me."

## Discography As Archaeology

But 4:00 P.M. didn't actually rediscover "Sukiyaki." Surfing through online shopping sites turns over all sorts of rocks. Cover versions of the song appeared almost immediately, first by The Ventures, who filled out albums featuring their original instrumental single hits with Fender Stratocaster covers of Top 40 charters, including "Sukiyaki." For obvious reasons, most early covers of the tune were instrumental and the song was eventually abandoned to the curatorial custody of stubborn survivors from the programmatic Trad Jazz of the Fifties, antediluvian musical thugs like Billy Vaughan and Kenny Ball, whose generic Easy Listening Orchestra arrangements would torment elevator occupants and department store shoppers for decades to come.

Credit for re-animating the song should probably go to the young star of Tejano music, Selena, whose life and career were tragically shortened by an obsessed fan club president who shot her dead in 1995. Selena came from a musical family and they have a lot of oldies stations in the Tex-Mex Bean Belt. She was moved by the song to write her own transliteration into Spanish for her 1989 album, *Selena*. The website www.webjefita.com publishes both her Spanish lyrics and an English translation. While she stays true to the theme of lost love, her lyrics are more emotional, less imagistic than the original or the 4 P.M. versions. The 4 P.M. quartet, led by the Pena brothers, Ray and Roberto, likely got the idea to cover the song from Selena.

Some truly weird covers exist. King Curtis Ousley, legendary R&B sax-master and studio musician riffed on the song, as did such diverse units as The Wicked Picketts and the Amos Garrett/Doug Sahm blues trio in a live recording at the Quatro Club in Tokyo in 1991. "Sukiyaki" has been served up by purveyors of contemporary disco and 'on hold' music like The Cover Girls and "A Taste of Honey." There's even a reggae version by some raver named Sayoko on a Reggae Summer Splash 1995 compilation on the Radikal label. In 1994, even an old 'isn't he dead?' dinosaur, former gospel singer and one-hit wonder Jewel Akens ("The Birds and the Bees") covered the tune at the behest of his demonic masters at K-Tel Records. One of the more interesting covers is a jam recorded by three Japanese jazzmen taking back their song; Tatsu Akoi on bass, Paul Kim on buk and John Sagami on taiko at the Chicago Museum of Contemporary Art in 1998, released in 2000 under the title Basser Live (Asian Import). If you do internet-searches for "Sukiyaki," you'll inevitably encounter a large number of 'obsessive love' sites—incipient stalkers who simply post the lyrics of the 4 P.M. version, as well as some who post Selena's, in the name of some lost love they just can't get over. These sites waste a lot of online time, but in their way they are as poignant as the hastily scrawled final messages of the passengers on JAL Flight 123; a testament to the enduring power of this odd little misnamed pop tune.

## I Look Up When I Walk

1963 was a year that ended a month prematurely. On November 22nd, U.S. President John Fitzgerald Kennedy was assassinated in Dallas, Texas. Everybody remembers where they were when they heard the news, but almost nobody felt the paradigm shifts that were coming. At the most basic level, the pop music jukebox of a more innocent time was about to have its plug pulled and its coin-box jimmied. One of its favourite front men of the moment, Del Shannon, whose hits "Runaway" and "Hat's Off to Larry" topped the international charts, was among the artists overshadowed that year by the improbable popularity of "Sukiyaki." Coincidentally, "Runaway" also referenced the rain=tears equation: "I'm a-walkin' in the rain, Tears are fallin' and I feel the pain..."

Like the Everly Brothers, Shannon was one of the Brylcreem-and-sideburns brigade, many of whom would bail out of rock into the more stable genre of Country & Western in the a-changin' times to come. But in the early Sixties, he and his ilk frequently toured Britain, where they were still popular among the neo-Edwardian Teddy-Boy hoods and aped by insipid wankers like Cliff Richard and greasy fakes like Adam Faith. Shannon, or someone in his entourage, caught a whiff of something new happening in the British scene and picked up a song there. In 1963, Del Shannon released his version of a song called "From Me to You."

Thanks in part to the dominance of "Sukiyaki," it tanked in the charts. But toward the end of the year, a DJ on a local Vancouver AM station—again, I'm 99% sure it was Red Robinson—aired a version of "From Me to You" by the British band who wrote it. It sounded like it had been recorded in an underground public toilet by four guys too drunk to play their instruments.

"That…was a band from England called The Bee-at-les," the deejay said in a bemused tone.

"Those guys'll never make it," I muttered, and turned off my radio.

TEN

# Last Call for Alcohol

January is the cruellest month in Vancouver, the Month of Failed Resolutions, but for Gordon Campbell, former Vancouver Mayor (1986-1993) and former Premier of British Columbia, (2001-20110), it's a full-on hoodoo when, unlike the romantic swallows of Capistrano, the ugly chickens come home to roost.

For instance, in January of 2019, London's *Daily Telegraph* reported that the Metropolitan Police were investigating a charge of sexual assault against Campbell brought by Judith Prins, a fifty-four-year-old Canadian woman who worked for the Canadian embassy in 2013. Campbell was then enjoying the considerable perks of being Canada's High Commissioner, a patronage plum handed him by former PM Stephen Harper. Prins advised her employers that Campbell had deliberately fondled her buttocks while following her up a stairway en route to a meeting. He did not apologize, as if it was an accidental contact, but acted like he'd done nothing wrong. After a "full due diligence investigation" by the Government of Canada—not the police—her allegations were declared to be "without merit," though she was told by Consul General Mark Fletcher that three other women had complained about Campbell's 'inappropriate behaviour.' Encouraged by the Me Too movement, Prins finally did what concern for her job probably stopped her from doing in the first place; she went to the cops in whose jurisdiction the offence occurred.

Caressing a woman's bum without an invitation is an act some men of my generation might have thought was a suave move when they'd had "tee many martoonies," as our Dads used to say, but after fifty years of increasingly determined feminist political activism? Maybe Campbell's brain was rain-softened by his Vancouver upbringing, or maybe by another liquid he'd had at least ten years to learn to avoid.

## Book Him, Danno

In January of 2003, then Premier of British Columbia, Campbell, was arrested in Maui, where entitled British Columbians go in mid-winter to get away from the cold rain for a few weeks. He was charged with Driving Under the Influence, *Dee-Yew-Eye*, as they say south of the 49th in *Warshington* State, where paddy-wagon chasing lawyers advertise their skills at getting offenders cleared of such charges on TV channels we get in Vancouver. Drunk driving is just about the dumbest, most avoidable charge anybody, never mind a wealthy, privileged connected politician, can get busted on.

Just so you know: I'm not pissing on a midget here. I felt Gord's pain. Thirty years ago, I was caught operating a motor vehicle when my better judgement went for cocktails, by a couple of the mall security guards who failed the casting-call for the Police

Academy movies and cover their shame with the badge of the West Vancouver Police.

My reason, not an excuse, is that a woman at a dinner party took advantage of a brief moment of privacy in the kitchen to put her tongue in my mouth deep enough to do a tonsillectomy, rubbed her crotch against mine like a weasel in heat and whispered sexual fantasies of a submissive nature. Not reactions I usually provoke in the other sex. With a come-hither look, she excused herself after dinner to drive home. Faking a headache after a decent interval of ten minutes, I lit out after her with my foot to the floorboards and a raging stiffy I may have mistaken for the stick shift.

Speeding down a West Van hill to Marine Drive to cut her off, a cat or raccoon dodged out in front of me and I instinctively reefed the wheel and 360-ed the rear quarter panel of the car into a low retaining wall. I was so stoked on testosterone and adrenaline, I actually volunteered to take a breathalyser. I thought I was sober. I just wanted to get to her place before she masturbated and fell asleep. She remains, as they say, "the one that got away." Served me right to suffer for my sin of unbridled perverse lust.

Through the colourful dusting of donut sprinkles in his moustache, Constable Tubbalarde, (not his real name), who administered the breathalyser, told me I was one drink over the legal limit and charged me. It was a quiet night and my licence had a non-West Vancouver address. At the time, I was working as a bartender at Vancouver's Terminal City Club, an over-upholstered private downtown booze-can loosely based on the London dining clubs founded by English aristos, a place where the high and mighty could puke into their shoes or drink 'til they pissed themselves and sleep off the excesses of gracious living in the Club's euphemistically named Snooze Room, instead of being anally raped in the drunk tank at the Main Street police station.

"The rich are different," F. Scott Fitzgerald once told Ernest Hemingway.

"Yes," Hem snapped in riposte, "They have more money."

Two things I learned at the Club: 1) drunk vomit always smells exactly like drunk vomit, whether it started out as Chateaubriand and Chateau Margaux or Kraft Dinner and canned Kokanee, and 2) a guy staggering out of a chandeliered, white linen draped dining room with a huge stain spreading down the back of his Hugo Boss pants smells just as ripe as a stiff passed out with an empty jug of Blue Lizard cooking wine in a Powell Street doorway.

Members, many of whom lived in West Vancouver, routinely left the Club pickled as barrels of herring to drive home. If they made it over the Lions Gate Bridge before their Mercedes or Caddys were pulled over by the Constabulary of the Duchy of Amblesnide & Tiddlycove, *they* got a 24-hour suspension and a complimentary ride to their door. No lights or sirens, of course. Barbarians from other municipalities were crucified along Marine Drive.

I fought the charge in court, but never believed for an instant my East End criminal lawyer could dance to the Muzak in a West Vancouver courtroom. We lost, which is to say, I got fined, lost my licence for six months and my lawyer got paid anyway. Lots of lawyers were Members of the Terminal City Club, but they either practiced corporate law or attached themselves, like parasitic remoras, to the predators who manipulated stocks on the infamous Vancouver Stock Exchange, taking options in lieu of fees for services rendered keeping their hosts inside the wide mesh of what passed for legal regulation in that shark tank.

Being a lawyer is like being a weatherman or stockbroker—one of those covetable jobs where you get paid even when you're wrong. Lawyers who invest in good kneepads and a case of lip balm can get themselves appointed to the Bench, which is not the hard slat implied by its name but actually a comfy, ergonomically designed chair. A couple of months after my conviction, I watched the judge who sentenced me drink a three-double-martini-lunch at the next table in an upscale burger-bar in North Vancouver, before *driving* back to the Bench in West Vancouver to sit in judgement over another line-up of remorseful drunk drivers. It was all I could do not to yard his chicken-legged ass out of his Lincoln Town Car, chain-whip the hypocritical butt-rag and toss him in a dumpster full of rancid fryer fat.

## Six Real Drinks

I don't know what Gordon Campbell's excuse was for driving after what the Mothers Against Drunk Driving (MADD) estimate was "14 regular drinks" (read: six *real* drinks). His wife had already returned to Vancouver. Why was he foolishly determined to drive 17 km back to an empty condo when he could have flopped on someone's couch? Six real drinks is more than double the amount required to make men start thinking with a part of their anatomy that, from childhood, they spend far more time stimulating than their brains. Campbell is said to be a martini drinker. As an expert witness who has sworn the Bacchic Oath on a stack of Bartenders Guides, I can testify that no beverage devised by the mind or hand of the mixologist acts with such deleterious effect on human judgement as the Martini.

Gin or vodka with a whisper of vermouth, stirred over ice. Ian Fleming was a pretentious twit—no true martini is shaken. A slipper of what amounts to three to four ounces of straight spirits, the martini takes the freeway to the brain with a detour through the libido. A couple of rounds of martinis can lower the collective IQ of a roomful of men quicker than the appearance of a peeler on the stage. Nor are martinis gender-specific. They're nick-named "panty remover" for good reason.

A cocktail waitress I'd worked with for years, whose romantic history I knew in detail and whose friendship I esteemed, drained several one night before we went back to her place for an innocent nightcap. She excused herself to "change out of her work clothes." When she came back to sprawl on the daybed in an ensemble of peach-coloured lace, camisole and matching loose French knickers, I knew better than to assume my charm and good looks had won her over at last.

## The Politics of Drinking

No evidence of motive beyond mere stupidity, itself an interesting indictment, emerged in Campbell's case, though veteran newspaper hacks must have sniffed the sheets. Campbell had enough of our money in his pockets to buy a cab, or a cab company, if he'd had a mind left to do so. Drinking martinis, it's all too possible he didn't.

Back home, Campbell went on TV, snivelled and apologized to everyone in general, then subtly shifted the blame to his father, asserting he too had experienced the devastating effects of Demon Rum on the family. It's always illuminating to watch politicians in crisis. They have no sense of shame. They'll say and do *anything*, however humiliating, transparently false, self-serving and hypocritical, as a preamble to announcing their decision *not* to resign their office because "the people" gave them a mandate.

Understandably, they don't identify the actual "people," (not to be confused with the electorate), who bankrolled their candidacy on the promise of preferred place cards at the trough and who'd be seriously pissed if the guy they've made their Bitch suddenly went coy and hetero in the showers. Campbell had no choice but to ride out whatever corrosive scorn the media and the people he claimed to represent heaped on him.

No doubt he'd have preferred to be almost anywhere but in front of those news cameras, demonstrating the hypocrisy of all his calls for resignations of NDP government ministers for the slightest audible fart of scandal while he was leader of the Opposition. He'd rather have been home, phone off the hook, under his blankie with a soother and a quart of Tanqueray to dip it in. In his place, I would have. But a decision to resign out of respect for the office he'd disgraced could have ruined him—financially, socially, even fatally.

Campbell's candidacy and election were bought and paid for by the business elite of British Columbia, who perennially conspire to keep control of the Legislature in the hands of toadies and lickspittles who will compliantly lubricate the bowel movements of commerce with lots of enthusiastic tongue. I know because I was their bartender during the years when Campbell's accession to power was plotted over bottles of single malt, Chivas Regal and Tanqueray gin. When I said *fatally* in the previous paragraph, I wasn't hyperbolizing. I was present when some young brokers on the Vancouver Exchange boasted of having contributed to a $10,000 fund to purchase an open contract for the murder of *Vancouver Sun* investigative business reporter David Baines, who specialized in giving them Atomic Wedgies in print.

## Members of the Club

The TCC's 1000 to 1500 members are the top scum on the pool of banking, shipping, mining and brokerage industries that actually run the Province. There are similar "affiliate" clubs, many of them older, in every major city in Canada. In the 1980s, I watched an obviously Jewish New Yorker, guest of a Member, tear into the regulars at the Fellowship Table in the men-only bar. "You assholes wouldn't have let me in the fucking front door ten years ago!" He still couldn't get a membership in certain Vancouver golf or yacht clubs frequented by TCC members.

The TCC began admitting Japanese, Chinese, and Korean businessmen as Members in the late 1980s, chiefly because it is above all a *business* club and money farts loudest in any room. Despite silly rules against business papers on tables in the bars and dining rooms, briefcases checked in the cloakroom, more deals get done in the Club's lounges and billiard room than in any boardroom in the city.

There are no politicians among the Membership unless they are independently wealthy. Politicians are occasionally treated to a glimpse of the inner sanctum as Guests. It was amusing to watch Grace McCarthy, Bill Vander Zalm and even some surprises like former NDP Premier Dave Barrett, flashing nervous shit-eating grins as they tip-toed through the labyrinth of bars and lounges like creeping felchers in a bathhouse, unsure whose ass to stick their tongues up. Inside the Club, politicians are *servants*, barely a cut above the bartenders and stewards who bring the drinks.

For supposedly astute businessmen, at least according to their resumes and corporate salaries, the Members have made some stunningly stupid deals with the Devil when backing 'free enterprise' candidates for Provincial Premier. Bill Bennett, son of Provincial godfather WACky Bennett, was later exposed for insider trading in Doman Industries. Bill Vander Zalm, the self-made Tulip King of Fantasy Gardens, accepted a paper bag filled with $20,000 in change from a foreign millionaire in a hotel room. Kim Campbell, a woman they hated but backed because she was smarter than any of the men in the room (no serious contest) had twice the ambition and guts, unfortunately also had twice the opinion of herself she was entitled to.

Gordon Campbell is a former Marathon Realty developer, whose grasp of 'free market capitalism' is based on exploiting the legacy of a monolithic real estate subsidiary created to develop lands granted *free* to a 19th century railroad company, in exchange for linking the country's coasts by rail. The CP/Marathon lands comprise the downtown core of every Canadian city that owes its foundation stone to the railroad. How smart would you have to be to turn a profit on a gift like that over a hundred years? Would you even have to be awake? You certainly wouldn't have to be sober.

## Serving Them Right

The people Gord worked for aren't. To be fair, the majority of TCC Members use it only occasionally for business entertaining. But when I worked there, the hundred or so hardcore Members were drunk every day, some of them before noon, a lot more by 5 p.m. By nine or ten at night the language and behaviour in the men-only upstairs grill room was as ugly as in any low tavern I've been barred from. I used to open the bar at 10 a.m. to a small crowd, a dozen or so Members who had offices in the building above and dropped down in the elevator when their secretaries went on coffee breaks. I learned not to embarrass them by asking them to sign for bottles or mixes until they'd discreetly downloaded a quad shot of their poison of choice to steady their hands.

The Club has an old non-conforming licence that allows it to sell wine and liquor by the bottle at the liquor store price, plus a small corkage fee. Members have private lockers that hold up to seven bottles of hooch. Despite the decor, which in my time looked like it had been acquired at an auction of 1960s Las Vegas casino furnishings, the place is just a booze-can, a speakeasy purchased-politicians turn a blind eye to on account of the collective influence of the Members.

When the BC Government sent its flunkeys around to make the bar staff jump through hoops to earn the Serving It Right card they decided every waiter and bartender must possess, we laughed in their faces. How do you police the liquor intake of clients who have keys to personal lockers containing enough joy juice to get a chapter of the Hells Angels through Happy Hour?

Cheap booze in deluxe surroundings. The rich stay rich mostly by paying less than the rest of us for everything, from interest rates to cocktails. That's why they have money left overt to get people like Gordon Campbell and his squalid ilk elected to office. The job of these retainers is to "maintain a business-friendly environment," or if you like, to grease the skids that enable certain people to make more money than you or I could contemplate without doubling down on the Prozac. Some Members serial marriages seem to have been arranged by bank managers moonlighting at the Equity Dating Bureau. Members don't actually sell their mothers—that is an irresponsible canard. They merely leverage their mothers' assets. However, like cannibal sewer rats, they *do* eat their young and the weak, especially in the brokerage business.

## Where the Elite Meet

Two promoters of "junior mining stocks"—(Moose Pasture Mines, to quote *Financial Post* editor Diane Francis' hilarious scathing book, *Contra-preneurs*)—friends for more than twenty years: One retired, turned over his business to the son he groomed to make a living by being a lying two-faced sack of shit like his old man, a promoter so devoid of scruple he'd tout speculative stocks to employees of his club. Hustling Club waitresses for sex was frowned on but condoned if it was discreet. A few gold-diggers on staff successfully reversed this game and married enough money to make divorce a viable business, God bless and keep them. But hustling waitresses out of the savings they earned with fallen arches and varicose veins is an act so contemptible Lucifer may have to consult the big book of Ordinances of Hell to choose the appropriate punishment for these subhuman bog-monsters.

A promoter who used to do this came to the bar one day, livid at his long-time best friend, a notorious operator of "boiler rooms," in which wannabe brokers are hired to cold call senior citizens and the chronically gullible, usually from lists obtained by questionable means, to sell them a poke whose pig always seems to vanish due to "market forces."

"Can you believe it? As soon as my son took over the business, that prick tried to take it over behind his back!"

Could I believe it? Don't make me laugh, I might spill my drink. They snubbed each other in the grill room afterwards. I expect they kissed and made up when they found themselves chained to adjacent oars in the bilge of Lucifer's yacht, plying Lac Brimstone on an indefinite cruise. They'll have lots of their own kind for company. Like the guys who neglected to tell one of their fellow viral life forms, who lived off these timed junior stock scams, about the blow-off date for some roll of ass-wipe and left him holding enough worthless paper to stock his bathroom for decades, just like the members of the public who bought into the Initial Public Offering of BS Minerals.

Let's not forget the slimeballs who bragged about hiring 'talent' from temping agencies rather than employing permanent secretaries, using professional office service agencies as if they were escort services, buying the girls fancy dinners and too many drinks to stun them before the inevitable sweaty hand up the skirt and the pounce. I was the guy who wiped those girls snotty, teary faces with a cool cloth, poured brandy into them and helped them into a cab, before going back to mop up the puddle of puke. There are worse jobs than bartending. One of them is being a dry cleaner on Monday morning.

## See You in Hell

In March of 2003, the *Vancouver Province* reported that the second wife of one of my least favourite rye-and-coke soaked Members had been arrested for conspiring to have him murdered in Melbourne, Australia. Considering the things this loudmouth used to say about his first wife in the Club, I'm only surprised *she* never tried to have him whacked or simply cut off the flaccid dick he loudly bragged of making her suck for hours every night after going home cooked as a boiled owl. That's not the kind of thing you want to know about a woman while you're serving her drinks and dinner, though it does go a long way toward explaining her expression as she faced her husband across the immaculately laid table.

If only she'd asked one of the compliant Servants of the Club, *Would you please kill my husband?* We could have arranged to top off the rye bottle in his locker with something that would have solved her problem within minutes or hours, depending on the degree of agony she required. We would have done it with our customary discretion and impeccable tact. Service, as the Manager used to remind us, is what the Club is about. We could have saved her and Wife Two a world of trouble.

I'm looking forward to Hell. Members of the Club will recognize me. I'll be the horned, fanged demon with the whip studded with white-hot nails. I'm really going to enjoy hearing you tell me once again that I was the greatest bartender in the world and how you were going to open a bar and have me manage it, especially since you'll be repeating this patronizing drivel in a falsetto shriek of eternal *extremis*. Did I mention the red-hot branding irons shoved up your ass by abused former waiters and busboys? The white-hot castrating knives wielded by former waitresses and secretarial temps? Never mind. You'll find out soon enough. See you in Hell, you witless pricks.

From the Bloody Mary breakfasts and 10 a.m. coffee break rye-poppers, to the four double-martini power-lunchers, the corporate executives whose blood is 40% alcohol by volume at any given time of day, and the brokers who from 1 p.m. on, sit at tables strewn with bottles of booze and liqueurs, among the remains of an indifferent lunch consisting mostly of $100 worth of wines, wreathed in the smoke of $30 Cohibas, surrounded by a hobo-jungle of disbarred lawyers, failed promoters, and brokerage groupies suborned to "wash trade" their worthless stocks—these are the men who got Gordon Campbell elected.

Is it any wonder he drank? Who could wade in that kind of morally rancid human effluent for five seconds *without* a drink?

## Name Your Poison

Ganymede was the cup-bearer of the Greek gods. As a bartender at the Club I felt more like Charon, Ferryman of Hades. I learned it's not only possible, but relatively easy for a human being to consume more than a quart of distilled spirits in a day without becoming noticeably drunk, provided you start at ten in the morning. The only drawback is that after four decades of doing this every day, your liver is the size and consistency of a bowling ball and you die. During my last years there, many of the hardcore Members were becoming extinct as retirement enabled them to start drinking earlier in the day and cumulative liver failure cancelled their reservations with the Golden Years cruise line.

What most people know about alcohol they learn first-hand, which means they know jack-shit, since loss of judgement and skewed perception are conditions of the experience. This explains the infinite mystique drink has for the drinker. Bartenders see it differently because their job is to get people drunk while remaining sober, at least in your better class of establishments. I can't answer for the low dives you drink in, but I recall the days when waiters at the old Avalon beer parlour would take you at your word when you said "Have one for yourself" and drain a ten-ounce glass off the tray right at your table instead of pocketing twenty cents.

Alcohol kills more people than tobacco and quicker, especially if you factor in deaths due to drunk driving. Yet it remains the legal drug of choice in our culture, surrounded by a mythic effulgence of sophistication, as if there's some qualitative difference between a wine snob smacking his lips over a vertical tasting of a dozen top vintages of Bordeaux, a connoisseur savouring a selection of single malts at a "scotch bar," some metro-sexual swilling his way through the novelty martini menu at an industrial chic downtown bistro and a rummy sucking Sterno through a sock in a boxcar.

Put all of the above at the same table and after three rounds they'll be best buds. After four, they'll have solved all the problems of the world with the loudly slurred certainty of liquid genius. Rich or poor, savant or moron; drunks are all alike. Alcohol is the great leveller, the true solvent of democracy. Theocracies of any stripe, Islamic or Puritanical Christian, forbid its consumption for precisely this reason. Since banning it failed to do anything but intensify its mystique when the Americans tried Prohibition, we've had to create a complex mythology of connoisseurship around alcohol, reinforced by dress codes, pricing and membership in private clubs, to keep the guy with the bagged jug of cooking wine and the CEO with his single malt at separate tables. Managing the mythology of alcohol to keep the essential lubricant of our culture flowing smoothly without dissolving the social-class membranes is the job of marketing and advertising professionals who usually drink mineral water and decaf coffee.

## You Are What You Drink

What you drink tells people who you are and where you're from. Except in the rum-drinking Maritimes, rye whisky is the traditional Canadian spirit. Its manufacture is one area in which Americans acknowledge our superior expertise by calling our proprietary ryes, Canadian Club, Seagrams V.O., Crown Royal and a few others, *Canadian Whiskies* to distinguish them from American rye, which is something you'd serve to your mother-in-law or a tax lawyer if you had any left over from poisoning man-eating weeds in the yard. Corn-liquor is the true American whisky. Called Bourbon by law in Kentucky, and Tennessee Whisky over the crick from which Mr. Daniels' descendants have come to dominate the American market with JD's Old Number 7 Black Label. In Canada, rye is still popular on the Prairies and in small town bars—rye and seven, rye and ginger, rye and coke, rye and water, even shots of rye. Over the last four decades urban sales have nose-dived in favour of scotch, especially imported single malts, as if a shot or two of one of them would magically make you as suave as a Grenadier Guard in a shirt ad.

The true King of the Spirits for the last forty years has been the refined Russian moonshine we call vodka. People who insist on drinking 'authentic' Russian vodkas like Stolichnaya or Moskovskaya mystify me. These bottles come with caps made of such shoddy foil they can't even be screwed back on properly. Would you really want to drink something produced by a culture that can't make a decent bottle-cap? Or assumes you will have no further use for a cap once the bottle is open? Think about it. They probably filter that shine through old Red Army truck radiators. Drinking Russian vodka is like drinking Mexican beer. If my name was Juan and I made $4 a day brewing *cerveza* so a bunch of gringo yuppie fucks could pay $4 a bottle for it in Club Meds in *my* country, surrounded by walls and armed guards to keep *me* out, I know what I'd do in those vats, *cabron*.

Colourless, odourless and essentially tasteless, thanks to triple distillation and charcoal filtering, domestic vodka is the secret base from which bartenders launch their revenge on the drinking world. We mix it with Clamato juice, a concoction which resembles a blend of fish-slime and blood, to commemorate the assassination of a Roman dictator. We mix it with Southern Comfort, Sloe Gin and orange juice so giggling "ladies night" hen-parties can bat their lights at a bored gay stud waiter and tell him they'd love a Sloe Comfortable Screw. We mix it with pineapple juice, cream, ersatz coconut milk powder and pump six Pina Coladas into young girls in nightclubs so young men can acquire some questionable pre-marital experience.

When I drank seriously, I drank vodka—a straight shot splashed in a short wide Old Fashioned glass filled with ice, topped off with cold water. My mother warned me off mixed drinks; "If you're going to drink liquor, drink it with water." It turned out to be good advice to counter the dehydrating effect of alcohol, aggravated by mixing it with sugary sodas. My uncle Bill, who drank rye and water, blamed his occasional hangovers on "bad ice," never on the whisky.

Vodka and water is the ultimate drinkers' drink, stripped of taste, colour, bouquet, any pretensions that disguise the business at hand. Sometimes, when I'd had just enough, I felt I achieved the cool neutral transparency of the spirit itself. Like most things, it was a matter of fine measurement and timing. I once knew a rounder whose girlfriend was a junkie whore. Sometimes he'd use her outfit to crank a few cc's of vodka straight into the line and get instantly shit-faced. That was a matter of fine measurement and timing. A c-hair too much, you'd be instantly dead. You could spin a bottle of vodka out that way when you were between pogey cheques and the Duchess was too wasted to drag her ass down to the Penthouse, but it wasn't drinking.

## Drink, Drank, Drunk

Whether you're a purist draining a shot of Everclear, a guy downing sleeves of cold lager after work, or a *Chevalier du Tastevin* slurping up all the Chambertin your liver can hold, the end result is the same. You get drunk. Pixilated. Loaded. Sozzled. Smashed. Gunned. Shit-faced. Why do we do it?

Never mind the dumb things you do *when* you're drunk—trying to fuck people other than your significant other, picking fights with your best friends or total strangers twice your size and yes, *driving home.* The after-effects of getting drunk suck; a headache measured in megatons that causes you to move your head as gingerly as a truckload of old dynamite sweating in the sun; alcohol gastritis, which is like having a starved rat eat its way out of your innards and, if you persist, full-on delirium tremens, being trampled by Dancing Pink Elephants.

As a professional bartender, I believe people drink because being loaded temporarily alleviates the anxiety they feel in the face of experiences they can't control or don't understand, whether those experiences are professional, emotional, financial or existential. Being drunk—not knee-walking, slobbering-on-strangers drunk, but dispassionately, deliberately and decisively drunk—makes things seem to make sense, especially things that usually don't.

We'll do almost anything to get the feeling that things make sense—get out of a warm bed and go out into a cold world to jobs we hate every day, get married, have children, plan holidays, join clubs and political parties, pay our bills on time, save for our retirement. If things still don't add up, some of us will subscribe to Byzantine conspiracy theories involving the CIA, the Tri-Lateral Commission, the military-industrial complex, aliens in UFOs, Zionists, Freemasons, and The Pope. In desperation, a few will join cults, become Ku Klux Klansmen, Scientologists, born-again Christians or Satanists.

Most of us, in our lazy unimaginative way, opt for the handy remedy that's as old as civilization. We get drunk. It usually works. Getting shit-faced, going on a toot, a bender, a binge, gets us through the crisis until the shrink-to-fit rationales we live by kick in again. So far, alcohol is the closest thing to a panacea we've come up with in about ten millennia. People who become captains of industry or politicians recognize that alcohol enables them to make economic and political decisions whose implications would paralyse a sober person.

If Campbell was a mineral water sipping vegetarian who slept the sleep of the just after spending his decade as Premier closing hospitals while people died on waiting lists for surgery, privatizing government services and freezing the minimum wage to reduce even more people to poverty or near serfdom, all just so the wealthy folks who bought his election could get even richer and roll in deluxe private hog-wallows like the Terminal City Club, he'd be as easy to hate as Heinrich Himmler. If Campbell drank 'for effect' to endure the Devil's Bargain he made with the rich thugs he's shilled for and toadied to, it might argue for mercy on his sad, sold soul. But after all he's been through—his father's alcoholism, his DUI conviction and disgrace—evidence that he still thinks he's entitled to sing along with the late Amy Winehouse, *"Ain't goin' back to rehab, baby"* while riding the Canadian taxpayer gravy train and grabbing any woman's ass just because he feels like he's entitled to, indicates that he's incapable of learning from experience.

The Decline and Fall of Gordon Campbell is more than just the story of one flawed man. Campbell is a product of a culture of entitlement based on wealth alone, which views political power not as a social responsibility, but merely as a lubricant in an orgy of self-enrichment and gratification, a culture that has failed to learn from it's mistakes. Even a drunken glance at history is enough to indicate that failing to learn from your mistakes is a counter-evolutionary trait.

ELEVEN

# Roadkill

When this "Modest Proposal for the Wildlife of North Vancouver" appeared, Andrew McCredie, Editor of the local paper who published it was barraged with incendiary mail and irate phone calls from animal rights activists and ordinary folks who feed the birds and squirrels in winter and were righteously appalled by what they'd read under my byline. For whatever damage I inflicted on the circulation and advertising sales of *The North Shore Outlook*, I am heartily sorry and despise my sin. As McCredie noted, when stung to respond in print to one of the more vituperative missives: "It's obvious that the appreciation of the art of satire is as dead as the Latin language and the dime cup of coffee..."

Back before *Esquire* was more than a fashion magazine, I used to read it just for Jim Harrison's columns about "eating wild." With drool dripping from my chin, I'd groan as he described stuffing wood pigeons with fresh juniper berries and wild chestnuts or pan-searing thin strips of fresh venison in red wine to nibble with cuts of sourdough hot from the ashes of a campfire. In retrospect, it occurs to me that Harrison may actually have been writing his paeans to the joys of eating real fresh killed varmints stuffed with pine nuts and wild berries while chewing on his own specialties, Tongue in Cheek and Pulled Leg of Fool—coming soon to the freezer case at your local Food-Mart.

## Squirrel X-ing

One of the charms of living on Vancouver's North Shore is the abundance of wildlife, often literally on the door step. The first time squirrels scamper along branches, like Walt Disney's classic Chip 'n Dale, into the bird-feeder to steal sunflower seeds, or you surprise a family of raccoons on the back porch dining out of the dog's dish, it's cute. When you get the vet bill for repairs to the dog or cat after the inevitable dispute over place cards and dinner protocol, or when the raccoons smorgasbord your household garbage across the front lawn and rip up the roof shingles to move into your attic, those sweet little bandit-masked faces lose a lot of their Disney appeal.

Likewise, the explosion of the squirrel population on the North Shore in recent years has added a new variable to the increasingly crazed urban traffic pattern. Squirrel X-ing signs aren't likely to be posted by the municipality, since you'd need one for every ten feet of street, but the unexpected glare of brake lights as the car ahead suddenly slows and swerves to avoid squashing a jay-walking rodent has become a familiar hazard, a cause of rear-enders for which the driver following is almost always judged at fault.

Would any driver do as much for the squirrel's first cousin, the rat? Not likely. But squirrels and raccoons have been anthropomorphized to a level of cuteness that causes the stomach-flip reaction to a sickening thump under the wheels on a dark street, which usually means you've run over some kid's pet cat or dog. The honest light of day reveals many more Michelin-tenderized squirrels and entrees of Raccoon *a la Bonne Anée* than Pirelli *pâté* of domestic pets.

## The Chef's Special

My neighbour in Squamish was the Executive Chef at the Whistler Conference Centre when he got his first deer. Jean-Pierre is no hunter. An affable cosmopolitan French chef, he was driving to work when a deer launched itself out of the brush around Alice Lake to cross the highway, as deer are wont to do in the early hours of the morning. The damage a two hundred pound deer can do to the front end of a car is impressive, but Jean-Pierre expressed no regret at the near write off of his Ford Explorer. Chef to the core, he deeply mourned the waste of so much prime venison.

Like him, our frontier forbears would deplore the profligate waste of free-range animal protein caused by the automobile, especially when factory chicken and feedlot beef contaminated with antibiotics, steroids and possible mad cow disease or bird flu, command extortionate prices in shrink-wrap at the supermarket. It's even worse in Australia, where kangaroos behave like giant jackrabbits dazzled by the headlights of oncoming cars and night-driving big trucks called road trains, leaping into their paths. The backcountry highways of Oz are strewn with corpses of big Reds and Greys. Bleeding hearts from the cities eulogize the vehicular slaughter of a national symbol. Territorials just make sure their utes and trucks are protected by heavy roo-bars extending beyond the fenders to minimize the damage.

As a hungry tourist who has tasted medallions of 'roo in a red wine sauce, I shed a tear for the waste of all those delicious cutlets. My anthropologist brother Phil in Western Australia has eaten 'roo cooked whole *à la mode*, buried in a traditional pit of heated stones, though he admits he never had the discourtesy to ask whether the main course was dispatched with a boomerang, 30.30 or a Ford Holden.

I'm not suggesting we all start carrying a shovel in the trunk and give new meaning to the phrase, "I'll just run down and pick up something for dinner." Those posters you used to be able to buy advertising the fictional roadkill grill, with its motto, "You kill it, we'll grill it!" were novelties young men used to decorate their first bachelor quarters. In fact, roadkill is improperly slaughtered and unfit for human consumption. Mind you, I have eaten snack foods purchased from crossroads vendors in certain parts of the world that made me wonder if the realtors' mantra, "Location! Location! Location!" had some especially apt local significance.

## Cheap Date at the Meat Counter

Consider for a moment what bounty and variety a short, properly run backyard trapline could add to the family diet, not to mention a serious reduction of the most expensive part of the grocery bill. What could be more convenient than having dinner come to you? No more scanning *best before* or *packaged on* dates on labels we suspect conceal a multitude of sins, never mind the darker concerns about how the meat industry uses ground up offal and bone meal to produce protein-rich feed for animals not naturally carnivorous.

With backyard wild game, we're talking about guaranteed fresh today and as free range as possible, within the contemporary urban environment, a menu enhancement not without precedent in Vancouver. Since the Great Depression of the 1930s, Stanley Park grilled squab and Prospect Point pigeon pie have been staples for those living rough in its commodious forest, not to mention fricassee of Coal Harbour Mallard and even Roast Swan *du Lac Perdu*.

I'm talking about putting meat on the table without any of the traditional drawbacks to hunting or trapping your own food. No farking about in the woods with freezing rain dribbling down the back of your neck. No stiffening up in a blind, cradling a loaded shotgun for hours, or stalking in point blank underbrush, praying some similarly over-armed moron won't mistake you for a twelve-point buck.

A suburban trapline can be maintained from the comfort of a lounge chair on your covered patio or deck, within easy reach of sustaining infusions of espresso or cold beer and equally handy to the propane-fired Broil King when the snapping of sprung traps announces dinner is in the bag instead of a plastic filmed Styrofoam tray. A headshot from a small calibre .22 handgun or varmint carbine is the most efficient *coup de grace*, though bylaws against the discharge of firearms in residential areas make it problematic. Sensibly parsimonious with precious ammunition, pioneers would have used a heavy stick (or modern tire-iron) to finish off anything smaller than a wolverine anyway.

## The Joy of Cooking Varmints

As for preparation, you need look no further than the copy of the culinary classic, *The Joy of Cooking*, your mother gave you as a housewarming present when you moved into your first bachelor/ette digs. Pages 511 to 515 contain complete directions for skinning, dressing, and preparing small wild game for the table. Read them carefully, particularly the instructions for removing fat and glands, and wear rubber gloves to prevent highly contagious and occasionally fatal tularemia infection. Mouth watering yet?

Squirrels can be oven-roasted exactly like small birds, (think Cornish game hens), stuffed with a handful of grapes, sage, and chopped celery to be discarded later. Like any game, squirrel is very lean, so barding—wrapping the meat in strips of bacon—is essential to retain juiciness and flavour. Preheat the oven to 450 F, place your barded Nutkins on a rack above a roasting pan and give them the big heat for about five minutes, then lower the heat to 350 F for about fifteen to twenty minutes, depending on the size of the critters.

Another option to tenderize and prevent drying out while cooking is to melt a tablespoon of butter in a skillet, brown the squirrels as you would pieces of cut up frying chicken, then dip them in a sauce whisked together from a cup of orange juice, one quarter cup of honey, two tablespoons of lemon juice and a dash of salt and bake them uncovered in a 350 F oven for twenty minutes. At this point, turn Chip and Dale over, add a little fruit traditional in game cookery to the sauce—raisins, dried apricots, peaches, pears, or prunes, baste them with the sauce and cook for another thirty minutes. Serve with a mix of wild and domestic rice.

Squirrel Stew is a forgotten staple of the pioneer table. In the past, skill with a long-barrelled small calibre rifle was esteemed because a hunter had to be able to literally shoot the eye out of a squirrel at fifty yards to avoid obliterating the meat with a destructive body-shot. A well-seasoned cast iron Dutch oven is essential for this dish. Four or five squirrels, roughly a pound each, jointed as you would a chicken or rabbit, sautéed in a quarter cup of shortening starts the fun. Brown at least half a cup of chopped onions in the fat after removing the meat. Place the reserved squirrels in your pot with the onions and add two cups of skinned, seeded, and diced tomatoes, three cups of drained canned kidney beans, a cup of boiling water, and a pinch of cayenne or powdered chili to taste.

Simmer the lot, covered, until the squirrel is just tender, and add three cups of corn, ideally cut fresh from the cob. Fuss with the seasoning. Add Worcestershire or a jolt of your favourite hot sauce. Serve in bowls with fresh warm sourdough bread to mop up the gravy. Provide bandana napkins.

## Roast Rocky Racoon

Roasting a raccoon requires some prep time, a steady hand with a sharp knife and a strong stomach. After skinning and removing all the innards and fat, you have to make sure to remove the glands in the small of the back on either side of the spine, as well as the ones under each foreleg. Soak the raccoon, refrigerated, in saltwater overnight and hope no unsuspecting guest opens the fridge. Blanch in boiling water for forty-five minutes, add two tablespoons of baking soda and continue to cook for another five minutes. Drain and wash in warm water, then place in fresh cold water and bring to a boil. Reduce heat and simmer fifteen minutes while preheating the oven to 350 F.

You're still only half done. Now stuff the saddle with apricot-prune dressing, made by combining one and a half cups of mixed dried apricots and pitted prunes with four cups of dry bread crumbs or three cups of boiled rice, season with a quarter cup of melted butter, half a teaspoon of salt, an eighth teaspoon of pepper and half a cup of mixed chopped celery, parsley, and cilantro. Moisten the stuffing with a little stock or red wine. Bake the varmint in a covered roaster for about forty-five minutes, then uncover and bake an additional fifteen to twenty minutes, basting with pan juices. If this all seems like a shit-load of work, console yourself by imagining the looks on the faces of your dinner guests when you tell them what they're eating. Serve with winter vegetables—squash, carrots, parsnips and turnips. Don't throw away the coonskin. Take it to a taxidermist and he'll whip you up a fine Davy Crockett cap to replace that sissy chef hat your wife bought you for when you're being The Man at the barbecue. If you're really smart, serve the fucking coon to your editors, creditors, and in-laws while you sneak the family out the back door and down to the A&W Drive Thru.

TWELVE

# Crash Test Dummy

There is no more sobering sight than a heap of metal mangled by speed and misadventure, especially when it's the wreck of a car you've coveted, a sleek steel missile you've imagined yourself piloting on a scenic winding highway with nowhere to go and all day to get there. In my case it was a wire-service photo of Peter Hommel's black beauty Audi TT roadster after he lost it in an autobahn crapshoot near Eisenbach in January, 2000. Hommel was a top-ranked German rally driver, a far better wheelman than I ever was or hope to be. The photo is the kind of you'll-live-and-he-won't crash porn certain cynical truck and SUV makers use to sell vehicles by appealing to our most basic instinct.

I'd been feeling certain secret middle-aged male yearnings. No, not *those*; the ones inspired by the new breed of roadsters like Hommel's TT, the BMW Z3, the Porsche Boxster, the Honda S2000 and the Toyota MR2. It started in the late 80s, when Mazda stunned the pundits with its cute little Miata, whose styling reminded ageing male fantasists of the Lotus Elan a cat-suited Diana Rigg drove as Emma Peel in *The Avengers* 1960s TV series.

While social engineers, scientists, and environmentalists were warning us daily about the depletion of fossil fuels and global warming, the importance of improved public transit and the development of electric or other alternatively powered cars, we went on a politically incorrect sports car buying binge. The Miata sold across the board: to old and young, to men and especially to women. Its success inspired higher-priced imitators to exploit a market made up of Boomers whose adolescent fling with sports cars left a residual itchy spot on the palms of their shifter hands.

These new sports cars aren't the British roadsters I loved even as they shook my teeth loose and tenderized my kidneys. Standard features now include driver and passenger airbags, power steering, anti-lock brakes and, at the high end, as in the BMW Z3, stuff with techno-whiz names like Dynamic Stability Control which counters skids "by applying individual brakes in a turn." You'd expect that kind of compensatory engineering in mass-market rides like the Oldsmobile Alero, which calls it the Active Response System, just as it figures Cadillac would come out with thermal night vision which sees beyond the headlights, since Caddy drivers tend to be of an age when one's own headlights aren't as bright as they once were.

Despite bragging up safety features in their promotional advertising, while powerful sports cars get to be like stealth fighters, piloted as much by onboard computers as by the guy at the wheel, the recurrent vogue for illegal racing on urban streets is taking the amateur rally to a new and deadlier level.

## Uncool Cars

I became a sports car buff by default. In 1968, being into cars was totally uncool unless you were a duck-tailed hood who drove a jacked '57 Chevy or one of the new generation of burger-cruisers—a Ford Mustang or Plymouth Barracuda. Among my peers, aged Cor-Vans, rusty Bedfords and the ubiquitous VW bus painted with paisley flowers, peace signs and Establishment-baiting slogans were the preferred mode of transport to Be-Ins, Love-Ins, and Trip Festivals. I fell out of the resinous shag-upholstered interiors of many a mobile stereo system-opium-den-shag-parlour, with the 8-track blasting Jimi Hendrix's *Are You Experienced?* to the neighbourhood, announcing the return of the prodigal at 5 a.m. Vans offered privacy convenient for experiments, social, sexual and chemical, but the communal nature of van life got old fast.

Clancy Gibson, an artist I knew who did posters for some of Vancouver's early underground clubs, had acquired a sacked out '56 MGA with a two-seat step-in cockpit as minimal as a First World War fighter plane. He took to wearing old bomber jackets and a leather pilot's helmet scavenged from a military surplus store. It rained the day he drove me to see a similar car going cheap. He'd thrown away the shredded canvas top when he bought the MG. The looks we got from other motorists as we cruised nonchalantly topless through a downpour, a couple of hard-asses sneering at the boys warm and dry in their Mustangs and 'Cudas, had me sold before I saw the car.

She was a faded red 1959 Triumph TR3A and I fell for her the way a punk cowboy falls for the first saloon redhead he sees after a long cattle drive. Her main bearings were shot, so she was mine for $150. For another $350, her engine was rebuilt by a friend's mechanic cousin, who did it on the sly to avoid discrediting himself with his hot rod clients. While he was at it, somebody stole the removed hood that had been left leaning against the outside wall of his shop. I went down to Coast Import Wrecking, then a scrap-yard in the shadows of the Granville St. Bridge, and found the best replacement hood in the place. It happened to be yellow.

I muttered something about not being able to afford a paint-job after the engine work. Clancy shrugged: "Red and yellow are now your racing colours."

With a copy of Jack Kerouac's *On the Road* in my pocket and quarts of 10W30 and Jim Beam under the seat, that car took me everywhere I wanted to go—the Okanagan, the Rockies on a whim, Big Sur, San Francisco, Marysville for pie and coffee at midnight, street-racing from Taylor Way to Horseshoe Bay in the late traffic-free hours of the aimless nights of youth. Cruising, always cruising, with just the wind and the low growl of the engine for company. She made me feel like we could have gone to the end of the world on a set of Michelin retreads and two fingers of premium leaded gas.

It wasn't long before we had a disorganized car club. TR3s and 4s, Austin-Healy 3000s that would leave any Corvette sucking fumes and burning rubber off the light, a handful of MGs, bug-eyed Austin Sprites, old Porsche coupes that were mostly Bondo, even the odd rust-ragged Jaguar 120. We tore up the streets of Vancouver, playing hare-and-hounds from one all-night cafe, like the old Sportsman on Dunsmuir, to another. As young men will, we drove too fast—often in self-defence after sliding up beside a Vette, Mustang, or Camaro at a red light and shouting, "Hey, do you prefer that pig wagon to a *sports* car?"

A thug-loaded big V8 red-lining behind you is a real impetus to master the fine art of weaselling, as we called threading a ton of metal through the shifting apertures of slower traffic at high speeds and hugging the inside line on corners too tight for Detroit iron to handle. Once you'd pulled the lugs and got a glimpse of the quaint 1930s brake components meant to stop your hurtling 2000 pounds of steel, it was clear your best chance of staying alive was to learn to heel-toe the brake and gas pedals, accelerate through corners and put your trust in the rattlesnake reflexes of youth.

## Stupid Old Cars

British automotive engineering in the late 50s and 60s was the nadir of low-tech, enlivened by elements as amusingly quirky as they were violently perverse. Except for the coachwork, cars were cobbled together using pre-existing components, like the ubiquitous erratic Lucas electrics that were a frustrating feature of all English cars, subject to fizzle without warning in wet weather. Like, it never *rains* in England?

Nobody has ever repaired English car wiring and remained sane. Mechanics would take one look at the rats-nest of multicoloured un-coded wires and rip the lot out with a snarl, tossing the rainbow knot in the scrap bin with a curt, "I don't have time and you don't have the money to pay me to fuck with *that* shit. I'll rewire it."

For the TR3, the first borrowed 1.5 litre mill they used didn't have the juice to move what was a heavy car for its class, so they lifted a two-litre block from a Vanguard farm tractor, slapped a pair of SU carbs on it and hit the jackpot. As for the carbs, when Clancy stripped his SUs and rebuilt them, he wound up with a hubcap full of leftover springs and unidentifiable widgets, yet the carbs ran sweeter than ever. Who knew cars had vestigial organs? You could adjust SUs idle and mix linkage with the same dime you used as a spare ignition key. My entire tool kit consisted of one long flat-head screwdriver, a small adjustable crescent wrench and a ratchet with a couple of sockets. I could take the car down to the frame, if I had to. Once or twice, I almost did.

Low-tech has its downside. Apparently only dwarves and elves worked as mechanics in Britain. It was easier to get your tool into a high school prom queen than to get a normal-sized wrench into places where things needed to be fixed on these cars. Seeping open sores on knuckles became a badge of fraternity. When you did get a wrench into a tight spot, you'd discover the builders used an eccentric mix of metric and imperial nuts and bolts in the assembly. At some point, in the middle of a job, after prolonged imaginative cursing, bloodied fingers and thrown tools, somebody would utter the dreaded words, "It must be a fucking *Whitworth*."

Whitworth was an archaic British size and thread pattern for nuts and bolts. Everyone who owned a British sports car swore they put in one or two Whitworth bolts just to fuck with you. Nobody, not even mechanics, had Whitworth-sized tools. They could only be removed by tortuous hand cranking with pliers, vice-grips or crescent wrenches, usually from positions no circus contortionist or yoga master would dare attempt. Whitworth was the ultimate gremlin among British sports car owners, our nickname for nemesis.

Steering wheels were big, response as direct as you could get short of a Grand Prix track. Suspension systems were a crude oxymoron on par with those of old rigid-frame Harley-Davidson motorcycles. Internal organs, especially kidneys, got pounded like schnitzel. A drive around the block would result in a foot race to the toilet or a charge of lewd exposure in the alley. Transmissions were tight, tolerances unforgiving. Mastery of the art of double-clutching was an essential pre-synchromesh skill, especially if you wanted to drop into second gear at 90 mph. She'd jump four feet sideways and burn rubber the hard way, but she'd hold together if you missed the light pole and the family station wagon in the oncoming lane. If you learned nothing else, you learned that these cars were very dangerous.

## Smarter Cars

By the '70s, sports cars had changed radically. When I test-drove a friend's mid-70s Alfa Romeo Spyder, already a decade out of date at the time, it relegated my old Triumph to the fossil record. The Alfa cornered on invisible rails. Its engine was so sensitive that Gino, the moody and expensive Italian mechanic who worked out of a shop near Powell and Commercial, asked you if you wanted it tuned for the city or the highway. *Scuzi?* Who knew engines could be so discriminating?

Driving the Alfa inspired my last bachelor fling with a sleek angular Porsche 914. I loved its efficient lines and the pop-off hardtop you could tuck in the trunk. I shopped carefully for one that had been converted to dual carbs, having been warned that the factory fuel injection system was the one used on early VW Rabbits, a piece of electronic shit I'd have smashed with a big rock beside the highway one hot afternoon if the Bunny in question hadn't belonged to someone else. You needed TV repairman's tools to adjust it. On that occasion I may have ranted at length and volume about the good old days when I used pocket change to adjust the Triumph's fuel linkage.

I learned my first lesson about smarter cars when I wheeled into a self-serve gas bar, needle on E, and pulled the release catch to access the front-mounted gas tank. The handle came off in my hand. The hood, which offered superb protection against siphoning or gas tampering, was now locked against anything short of a crowbar. Luckily I had enough fumes to coast to a mechanic. It took him two hours of non-stop cursing to pinch the lost end of the cable and pop the hood. The next step would've been to yank out the dashboard. By then he was ready to do it just for spite.

At least one military historian has observed that Germany lost the Second World War even though they had the best tanks because their designers, including one Dr. Porsche, re-invented almost every model from the treads up. On the battlefield, this translated into a scarcity of interchangeable parts cannibalized from wrecks and lots of heavy machinery left to rust in the big parking lot of the Russian steppes for want of a Panzer Mark IV Wurlitzer Valve.

"Too clever by half, those Jerries," said the Brits, grinding along in mass-produced Lend-Lease American Sherman tanks, under-gunned but durable as Model T's and fixable by any scavenging tanker with a crescent-wrench. I'd have traded my sleek *Fahrtwagen* for an MG Midget with less torque than an espresso grinder, even-steven, the day I couldn't gas up without a mechanic's help.

The U-914's five-speed gearbox had been designed with impeccable Teutonic logic. Reverse was forward left, not dangling in limbo as in British trannies. Other gears were backed up one position to form a neat geometric grid. It made perfect sense, except that it went against the brain-to-hand muscle memory of every veteran sports car driver. In the TR3, I knew what gear I was in from the tenor of the engine, the vibrations in my hip against the high transmission tunnel, the angle of my wrist on the stick and my fingers knew exactly where to go when the revs hit that redline scream. In the Porsche, I had to watch the tach and re-arrange my neurons constantly. It was like wanking with the other hand.

I spent shit-loads of money on *Portia*, as I came to call her, replacing her flimsy rocker panels with heavy gauge ones fabricated by a Dutch body-man for $200 rather than forking over $600 for foil wrap Porsche factory parts. I even had her dated 70s two-tone paint disguised with a single all-over coat of VW factory Rabbit beige, a close match to the paint of Erwin Rommel's Afrika Korps. I restrained myself from having small white palm trees stencilled on her doors. Yet in the end I was almost relieved to sell it to a Chilean playboy who already owned a dozen, including a rare 916 model loaded with the Targa engine.

"Because I know how you love your car and how it hurts you to sell her to me," Juan Carvahal said with effusions of Latino emotion—a weird mix of sentimentality and *machismo*—he offered to take me for a night-ride around North Vancouver in his sleek black 916. It was like being abducted by a UFO. I was grateful to get home with no memory of being anally probed.

## Speed Kills

The first automobiles were luxurious hand-built horseless carriages, toys for the rich. To sell cars to the mass public, manufacturers not only had to make them cheap, they had to make them exciting. They did it by sponsoring car races. Since the first pedal was put to the metal, the old *Mille Miglia*, the *Gran Prix*, Indianapolis 500, stock car races and straight drags have been heavily backed by the auto industry as opportunities for engineering research and especially as marketing tools. Racing fans may drive family minivans or gas-miser subcompacts, but high-performance car races remain as popular as ever and they sell only one thing—*speed*, and it's evil twin, *danger*.

Even contemporary television ads for many family sedans take the wolf in sheep's clothing line, hoping to appeal to the aging Boomer who wants to be able to drop off the wife and kids at the mall, then drive like he was back in his old bachelor MG or Mustang. Sedans and sports coupes are shown being driven, above a blurry subtitle stating "professional driver on a closed course," at fantastic speeds on dry lakebeds through rooster tails of abrasive sand. Like anyone would do *that* in a car that just cost him over seventy grand. Not to mention the ads that show cars on empty roads filmed at ordinary speed then speeded up or digitally back-grounded to create the illusion of perfect road-holding at *Star Trek* warp speeds.

The spate of Audi TT smash-ups that peaked in the millennial summer after the model was introduced began with three fatal crashes in addition to Hommel's, in the month of January alone. At the time, the TT was leading an Audi comeback after safety scares in the 80s over unexplained accelerations and experimental oil-filled shocks that caught fire had pretty much erased Audi from the roster of prestige cars in North America.

My original draft of this article implied blame for the accidents to questionable engineering by Audi, who were trying to dodge the bullet by retro-fitting the TT with a spoiler supposed to prevent future accidents. My editor at the *Vancouver Sun*, Jim Sutherland, a car buff himself, took the precaution of contacting a local Audi dealer who pointed out that several of the fatal accidents happened to professional drivers operating at the limits of control. He claimed he drove his TT the same careful way he did his VW Jetta—in other words, he drove it to show he could afford to.

Jim rewrote the penultimate paragraph to include the dealer's comments without consulting me. No doubt he was concerned about offending the luxury car dealerships who advertised in the paper, yet he was right in the sense that *I* should have made those calls myself to cover my ass before going to print. Just as well I didn't, since I'd only have asked them embarrassing questions about the history of Audi, part of a conglomerate called Auto Union back in the 1930s when, with Nazi government support, they pioneered radical mid-engine designs that produced very fast but also very unstable racing cars that eventually killed even the one German driver, Bernd Rosemayer, who seemed to have mastered them.

I quit driving like that a long time ago. The memory of my last fast night-ride is imprinted on my synapses. I drove my friend's Alfa Spyder along the winding Dollarton Highway to North Van from Deep Cove at speeds so high I couldn't risk checking the speedometer. I just put the hammer down and concentrated on keeping the car connected to the road. When I pulled over in the Lynnwood Hotel parking lot and handed back the keys, for the first time I thought about all the side-streets and hidden driveways along the route I'd just burned, the designated drivers or shift workers who could've pulled out into my rocketing path, elderly insomniacs who might've picked that moment to take Fifi for a late walkies, teenage boys legging it from girlfriends bedroom windows, the dogs, cats, raccoons, and existentially tortured souls who could have picked that moment to step out for a midnight rendezvous with fate.

James Dean died when he over-drove his Porsche Speedster head-on into a guy who was just dawdling along in a big chunk of Detroit steel. Whatever the loss to Hollywood, the right guy died. It doesn't always play that way. Around the same time I took my final fast ride, a girl I knew was dating a young man from a wealthy family and went on a road trip in his new $100K Porsche Targa, looking forward to some deluxe speed. She came home disappointed.

"He did the speed limit the whole way. I was waiting for him to turn it loose and he drove like my mother! He could *afford* it, but he didn't know how to drive it. He's afraid of his car."

At the time, I snorted contemptuously at the chequebook playboy, but improvements in technology in any area—cars, firearms, computers, or rock-climbing gear, can create delusions of enhanced ability in their users that are potentially lethal. Now I think that young man might have taken to heart Clint Eastwood's famous advice in *Magnum Force*, "A man's got to know his limitations."

I'm thankful I got to know mine without killing myself or anyone else. In 2014, the Morlocks who monitor such things announced that Vancouver's traffic was officially slower than that of Los Angeles, impervious to weaselling. These days, I drive a Volvo station wagon my wife calls Sven. Sven reminds me to fasten my seatbelt, automatically adjusts the seat to my leg length and the mirrors to my height. If I lit a cigarette, Sven would refuse to start and his dashboard display would remind me smoking is hazardous to my health. I suspect a robot arm might rise out of the console and snatch the offending weed out of my mouth. I'm okay with that. The last thing I need is a car that makes me think I'm a better driver than I am.

THIRTEEN

# Collecting for the Apocalypse

In the fall of 1962, tall grey sirens appeared among the firs of my North Vancouver neighbourhood and air-raid drills were held at school. I was twelve and having apocalyptic dreams. The headlines on the newspapers I delivered after school had gone from grim to apocalyptic: BLOCKADE! U.S. MOVES AGAINST CUBA! President Kennedy had accused the Russians of building missile bases in Cuba. Looking like a big bald evil baby, Premier Khrushchev threw a tantrum, whacking a table with his shoe, shouting, "We will bury you!" He didn't mean with a shovel.

Somewhere I'd read that Chinese emperors used to behead bearers of bad tidings. Every day I toiled up the steep streets of the Capilano Highlands with two sacks of the worst possible news slung like evil Pony Express saddlebags over my bike, but nobody tried to decapitate me. Instead, if the paper was late or I missed a house, I'd get a pink complaint slip on the top of my stack at the paper shack the next day and Rick, the sixteen-year-old sub-manager, would threaten to snip off my dink with the wire-cutters he used to clip the copper baling from the bundles. Two complaints and Frank the Manager came around to give me a blast. He was a man, at least twenty-years-old, who wore cheap sports coats and drove a small white car with *Vancouver Sun* on the doors in black gothic script. He made me sit in the front seat while he yelled at me.

"You got two complaints!"

I slouched in the hot vinyl seat, sulky and defiant. "I've got eighty papers. Everyone else has forty. I should be allowed four complaints."

"Don't crack wise with me, smart-mouth!" Frank screeched. "We'll split your route! You'll make half as much as you do now!"

"So split it. It's all uphill. Just give me the bottom half. One of them owes me for four months."

"Four months! Why don't you collect from him?"

"Because he never answers the door. He's got a bomb shelter in the backyard and he's in there all the time." There was a nuclear age "The Ant and the Grasshopper" story making the rounds, a rumour that people who had bomb shelters also had guns to shoot down their neighbours when *It* happened and everyone who'd snickered at them for ripping up the lawn to build the shelter came pounding on the lead-lined door to get in. I wasn't knocking on the door of anyone's bomb shelter—not for a year's subscription, prepaid.

Sometimes I dreamed I was still a paperboy after *It* happened and I delivered wads of blank newsprint to carbonized front porches, sets of cement steps that rose like primitive pyramids before heaps of radioactive rubble. Downtown there was a mountain of blackened concrete and warped steel where the Sun

Building had been and that was where the blank paper came from. I knew people still lived under where the houses used to be because the paper was taken in every day, but I couldn't collect because there were no doorbells left to ring and if I didn't collect Rick the Sub-manager, who had fallout cancer all over his pimply face, would snip off my dink with his atomic wire-cutters.

I didn't feel I could talk about these dreams with Frank. His indifference to headlines like RUSSIANS MOBILIZE! shouldn't have surprised me. Most paperboys just delivered the paper, they didn't read it. If the banner said WORLD ENDS TODAY! we'd have dutifully dropped it on every doorstep on our routes. Why would late-edition screamers like ALLIES BACK U.S. BLOCKADE! disturb our meditations about which girls in our class were getting breasts? Knowing a bit about Cuba and Castro was peculiar, I discovered, when our homeroom teacher asked us to tell the class who our heroes were. Most kids named hockey players like Boom Boom Geoffrion and Rocket Richard. A few of the brains said Dr. Banting or Winston Churchill. When she came to me, I foolishly confessed my admiration for Fidel. Miss Carey couldn't have been more appalled if I'd announced Adolf Hitler was my guy.

"But, John, Fidel Castro is a...communist!"

I knew that. I had a copy of *The Communist Manifesto* under my bed. Easy to swipe from the bookstore because it was so small, but the ideas in it weren't. In suburban North Vancouver people talked about communists the way they talked about strange men who tried to lure children into cars. I should have known better than to admit that, for me, there was something irresistibly honest about Fidel's wild beard and cigars and the way he wore plain combat fatigues when he could have ordered up any fancy uniform he wanted and awarded himself a chest-full of big shiny medals. I imagined what it would be like to be Castro's paperboy, delivering the *Havana Sol* or *Tiempo* to his house. I never pictured him in a Presidential palace, but always in some palm-shaded villa open to the sea breezes, like the photos I'd seen of Ernest Hemingway's house. I imagined him out on the patio, watching the sunset with a glass of rum, wreathed in cigar smoke, the kind of guy who would be less interested in the paper and the headlines he made than in talking to real people, like the kid who brought the paper.

My route ended at the treeline, where they were building more new houses to be added to my route if they didn't wind up premature ruins. Beyond, there were only mountains sheathed in thick fir and cedar forests, my Sierra Maestra. Along with *The Communist Manifesto*, the cabinets under my mate's bunk contained hoarded tins of peanut butter and jam, boxes of crackers, cookies, flashlights, batteries, candles, matches, Band-Aids, a small transistor radio I got for my birthday and a .22 calibre long-barrelled Colt revolver with two boxes of cartridges my Dad thought were still at the back of his bedroom closet on the top shelf. I had a plan. If the unimaginable happened and I survived, I'd take to the hills and come out when the glowing dust settled to create a new and better world.

## Rock Gardens of the Nuclear Age

Neighbourhood kids called the house I hadn't collected from in four months "the haunted house." The year before, it was just another typical post-and-beam, the Morden's house, but in the spring of '62 machines arrived, big yellow John Deere cats and backhoes. They clanked around behind the house to excavate a square pit that took up most of what had been the back yard. They were succeeded by a convoy of cement trucks. In the suburbs, that kind of activity meant only one thing. A swimming pool was the ultimate status symbol and everyone for blocks was talking about it, parents trying to recall if they'd met the Mordens at PTA meetings or cocktail parties or run into them at the Shop Easy. Kids were quizzed about how well they knew the Morden children. But the Mordens kept pretty much to themselves. Then the "pool" was roofed over, the exhumed soil bermed up over the roof and walls, revealing it for what it was—a blunt ziggurat of the Atomic Age, a fallout shelter.

Our school history book, immodestly titled *The Story of Civilization*, had pictures of ziggurats built in ancient Egypt and Mesopotamia—early types of pyramids, flat-roofed and stacked like steps. It looked like humanity's first form of monumental architecture might also be its last. Neighbours didn't see it so philosophically. Their disappointment about the pool turned to quiet outrage that by building The Thing, as it came to be called, Morden indicated he intended to sit out Armageddon with his family, presumably supplied with sufficient food and water and prepared to shoot down his less prudent neighbours.

The Mordens were ostracized. He was referred to as The Nut, and The Thing became the butt of tirades over burned steaks and jello-mould salads at pot-luck dinners, bridge nights, and cookouts. Morden made no attempt to disguise or beautify it, as some shelter owners did, planting heather and ground cover, as if their bunkers were just geometric rockeries. Worse still, once it was finished he stopped keeping up the appearances that are the central fiction of suburban life. Bulldozer tracks left the lawns looking like a tank parking lot but were never filled in, only hidden later by grass unmown for half a year.

By the time Mrs. Morden left with the children at the end of the summer, the pink paint on the cedar siding was streaked with green mould. The sundeck railings were grey, white paint peeling off like irradiated skin to reveal a skeleton of splitting two-by-fours. Part of the railing had fallen into the yard, but it didn't matter because nobody used either one anymore. I was the only person who knew Mr. Morden was still living there because I delivered the paper and it was taken in every day. I was afraid of his spooky rotting house, dark as a crime scene at night, but I kept delivering the paper as a symbol of the bond between us. We both knew something nobody else seemed to want to admit.

## Collecting for the Apocalypse

They had to face up to it a little bit more the day the papers I carried headlined: RCAF PUT ON ALERT IN CUBA CRISIS. OTTAWA TO SUPPORT U.S. ALL THE WAY. I imagined Fidel amusing his comrades by quaking in mock terror, "Madre Dios! Not the Canadians!" while cackling over the front page story that the UBC Engineers, famous for public pranks, had executed him in effigy before a firing-squad of water pistols. As I delivered to the Morden house, I noticed there was a light on inside. My collection book was in my bag with its wad of outstanding receipts, so I knocked on the door.

It snapped open immediately. Mr. Morden didn't look anything like I remembered. The collar of his shirt dangled around his neck like a loose noose, his pants were grimy and flapped around his legs above bare feet shoved into lace-less muddy brogans.

"What do you want?"

He sounded like Boris Karloff in a bad mood. Nervously, I explained that I was collecting for *The Sun*. Curtly he motioned me inside. The house smelled worse than stale. What had been the rec room was filled with piled up bags of uncollected garbage. The vestibule was a newspaper morgue. Papers were piled on papers, halfway up the walls in places, some obviously read, others with the front pages unturned, loose in tottering stacks like some demented archive of the last days of mankind. I only wanted to collect for four months, not for all of this.

"Four months!" He snorted contemptuously. "Four seconds is what we'll have." He glanced toward the back of the house as though calculating how many seconds it would take him to sprint to the sunken door out back, bar it and cock his shotgun. His agitation made me careful to avoid an accusatory tone. He gestured to the walls of newsprint surrounding us. "This tells nothing about what will really happen!" He began to thunder like a prophet. "There will be a shock like an earthquake! Wind like a hurricane of fire! Buildings will turn to dust in an instant! There will be nothing left of most people but shadows burned into collapsing walls! Skin will turn black and peel off like blistered paint! Flesh will melt like wax! Bones will turn to ash and be blown away before they can fall to the ground!"

His eyes glowed in the dimness like two pellets of plutonium. I held my collection book up in front of me like a pathetically inadequate radiation shield. It was the first time I'd met an adult who was insane. I'd been edging toward the door, but Mr. Morden went quiet as suddenly as he'd began to rant. Hauling a fistful of crumpled bills out of his pocket, he handed them to me. I told him it was too much, but he waved me off with an exhausted sigh.

"It doesn't matter...I know...I was there...I saw..." His voice was a ragged gargle.

I couldn't stop myself from asking quietly, "What did you see, Mr. Morden?"

His eyes glazed over in what we now call the thousand-yard stare.

His voice dropped to a whisper, "Nagasaki...August 8th, 1945...I was a prisoner of war...worked in a foundry near the city...I saw... I saw..." His eyes flickered, then dulled again. "Don't bring the paper anymore. No more...No more."

As I rode my bike home in the rain, I thought about his having seen the atomic bomb, which rescued him from slave labour and certain death, only to be haunted and hunted down by it like an implacable fury across two decades and thousands of miles to a disintegrating ordinary house on a quiet suburban street.

## The End of The End

The tensions of that summer and fall were swept away when a dragon of a storm, a Pacific typhoon, lashed the Northwest with its tail in passing. Wind-driven rain flooded the creeks of North Vancouver, washing out most of the old yellow wooden bridges like the one near the paper shack, whose creosoted support beams had been painted with apocalyptic Bible quotations by the anonymous vandal evangelists who defaced a lot of natural and manmade landmarks around Vancouver in the Fifties. Most of Vancouver was without power for twenty-four hours. Naturally that was the night I'd argued like a sea-lawyer to avoid the shame of having a babysitter and took charge of my brothers and sister for the first time when my parents went out to visit friends downtown for the evening. By 11 o'clock, when the lights died and huge trees began crashing down on neighbouring houses, I realized my parents weren't going to be home anytime soon.

Herding the frightened kids down to my room in the basement, I tucked them into my bed, raided my survival cache for candles and crackers, peanut butter and Fig Newtons and watched over them as they fell asleep while trees and homes exploded like bombs all around us. During nature's dress rehearsal for the end of the world, I sat up in a chair with the loaded Colt on my night table in case of looters, writing a long letter to Fidel Castro by candlelight, trying to explain how much I admired his refusal to back down to the Americans, but that I didn't want to die before I'd really lived or have to take care of three little kids in a postnuclear wasteland.

When my parents arrived home early the next morning, after being trapped in the botanical and automotive carnage of Stanley Park causeway most of the night, they made a big deal out of how well I'd handled the situation. It was easy to be modest because I'd been prepared for something so much worse. I'd hidden the gun and most of the evidence at first light. Later that day I slipped away and mailed my letter to Fidel. I didn't expect an answer. I figured from the headlines I delivered he had a lot on his mind: CUBA MANNING OWN MISSILES. DENIES RUSSIANS DOING JOB. U.S. WILL INVADE CUBA IF BASES STAY. U.S. REJECTS MISSILES DEAL. NO SWAP OF BASES. ALL AMERICANS READY FOR WAR!

Neighbours whose roofs had been crushed, windows blown out or back yards ripped away by floodwaters smirked at the news that a pump truck had been sighted at the Morden house. Supposedly an engineer, Mister Morden apparently knew doodle about drainage. The fallout shelter was flooded. A 'For Sale' sign appeared soon after and Mr. Morden disappeared from the neighbourhood forever. The house remained unsold and derelict for a long time. I only went back once, to make a final unpaid delivery when the paper announced: NIKITA TOSSES IN CUBAN TOWEL! WORLD HAILS JFK-NIKITA ACCORD! RUSSIA TO SCRAP CUBA BASES. ANXIOUS WORLD VOICES RELIEF AT EASE OF WAR THREAT. I knew he wasn't there, but I was going to live long enough to spend the money he'd overpaid me and I felt I owed him the gesture of bringing some good news to that sad house at last.

Recently I drove through the Capilano Highlands, surprised by how clearly I remembered which houses were conspicuous for their fallout shelters. I couldn't find a single trace of one, not even at the old Morden house, long demolished and replaced with a stucco monster home. They're all gone, bulldozed, filled in and forgotten by a new generation of suburbanites whose only worry is the state of their mutual funds. They live in the eternal present-perfect tense fostered by every facet of suburban design. No imminent mushroom clouds their blue-sky morning, blotting out the sunshine with the 'shadow of the valley of death.'

The treeline is higher now, thanks to the premium placed on view lots. My old route would have tripled, but the paper shack is gone and big daily newspapers have been gutted by 24-hour television news images that flicker across our consciousness to be instantly replaced with commercials. Kennedy and Kruschev are long dead. The Cold War ended in the 1980s and surplus nuclear warheads have been rumoured to be for sale on the international black market ever since. Old and ill, in 2006 Fidel handed over the country to his brother Raúl, one of the sinister figures in mirrored sunglasses and patent leather peaked fascist hats who used to appear behind him in photos. Raúl inherited a decrepit revolution, worn to the nub by five decades of vengeful U.S. economic policy that President Obama only belatedly, toward the end of his own final term, began to reverse. Fidel Castro died on November 25, 2016. He never answered my letter.

## FOURTEEN

# A 29 Hand

My Grandmother was the Cribbage Bitch. Oh, she was kindly old Nan while she taught us kids to play the strange card game we called Crib, the soul of patience as she showed us how to count our hands, making up two-point fifteens, runs of three cards, double runs and flushes, to hold a Knave in the hope of cadging an extra point by matching the suit of the cut card. She coached us endlessly in the strategy of pegging points during the first part of each hand when players lay down their cards one at a time up to the magic number, thirty-one.

Then, once we'd grasped the rudiments of the game, she proceeded to trounce us repeatedly and mercilessly. If she was within a few points of pegging out to win and we had yet to pass the Skunk Line at ninety points, she'd start sniffing loudly, smelling a skunk worth two games. If we missed counting a point or two in a complicated hand, she'd crow "Muggins!" and claim them herself, jabbing her pegs forward as if skewering small vermin. With the cards rippling in knitting-hardened fingers, she ceased to be Nan, my grandmother, and became an implacable nemesis— Minnesota Fats to my flawed Fast Eddie Felsen, Boris Spassky to my tormented neurotic Bobby Fischer.

I loved the game in spite of her and in spite of the game itself, which often seems over-complicated and dragged out by dull runs of the cards. "This isn't a hand, it's a foot," was a frequent complaint around the table when the deck went stiff and we struggled to make two or four points, tossing away our dealers bonus of discards with a muttered, "nineteen"—the zero hand in Crib—hand after hand.

I loved it because learning to play Crib was more than knowing a new game. It was an empowering rite of passage that earned you a seat at the big table with the adults, where there was no set bedtime and bowls of salty snacks. Peanuts and pretzels were not rationed as they were to kids watching cartoons on TV.

I still love Crib, but it's getting hard to find players among generations of people who grew up with Game Boys, Nintendo, X-Boxes and Net-linked personal computers. I may have to start trolling retirement homes for pigeons up for some insomniac post-bingo action. Cribbage is fast becoming a relic of camp bunkhouses, fishing boat galleys, Canadian Legion posts, and Friday beer night gatherings around Formica kitchen tables in parts of the country where the nightlife options are limited.

## His Nobs

The blue-collar associations of Cribbage seem odd, since the game as we know it was invented by the 17th century English aristocrat and poet, Sir John Suckling, (1609-1642). His father served King James I as Master of Requests, Secretary of State, and Comptroller of the Household—prime dispenser of patronage of his time, Chamberlain of Ye Olde Pork-Barrel. Small wonder he amassed a personal fortune and vast estates while in office. When he pegged out, Johnny, who was eighteen, got the lot. A handsome Cavalier courtier, Gentleman of the Privy Chamber to

Charles I, a poet and a dramatist who pubbed with Thomas Carew and Richard Lovelace, young Sir John was deemed by his peers to be "the greatest gallant of his time and the greatest gamester for bowling and cards."

It wasn't all claret and skittles. In 1634, Sir Johnny came home from doing his obligatory military training with Swedish King Gustavus Adolphus in his German campaigns, to discover a rival had skunked him for the hand of his beloved. Worse still, the Star Chamber's enforcement of the 1632 proclamation against the absentee landlordism that was ruining England's agricultural economy forced him to actually live on his estates, in the bloody *country*. Lovelorn, with slow rural time on his card-quick hands, Suckling picked up a rustic tavern game called Noddy, involving cards and a pegboard for scoring. Purely for fun, he transformed it into the game we call Cribbage or Cribbidge. Noddy lingers in the unique language of the game; the rhyming score-counts—"Fifteen-two and the rest won't do. Fifteen-four and the rest won't score," all of which Nan automatically recited like a nun repeating responses to the liturgy. In pegging, when "twenty-six" is called, you can't slap down a fin without hooting, "Five's a fix!" Twenty-seven is always answered with, "Four's in heaven!" The Knave on the cut or one in your hand matching the suit of the cut card, is "His Nobs," or "His Royal Nobs"—short for "a noddy Knave." *Noddy* is an old English word for idiot, as is *Muggins*, cried when claiming an opponent's uncounted point, which evolved into New World tough guy expressions like, "It's a mug's game."

Suckling escaped slow death from boredom in the boondocks by raising a troop of cavalry to enlist in the King's 1639 attempt to spank the ever-rebellious Scots, whose French conspiracies and homicidal allergic reaction to their national beverage made them an even greater danger to the English Crown than the Irish. The dandified uniforms and poor combat performance of Suckling's Horse provided comic relief in the otherwise disastrous campaign. Sir John still wasn't content to stay home, write verse-dramas, swill port and play Crib for the rest of his life. In 1641, he dabbled in the bungled plot to jail-break the traitorous Earl of Strafford from the Tower of London. After fleeing to France, his fortune forfeit, Suckling took his own life a year later.

## Mister Twenty-nine

After his death, his game returned to its proletarian roots and flourished. It travelled with traders and troopers of the Empire on which the Sun Never Set. The combination of sharp counting skills, strategic play, plus its length, (two games and a deciding rubber if needed), made it popular in far-flung military and commercial posts and 'tween decks on long sea voyages and patrols, where killing slow time is the true purpose of recreation.

No surprise, its strongholds are in former British colonies and possessions, especially where winters are long. New England, the Midwest, and the former Hudson's Bay Company "Oregon Territory" remain U.S. bastions of the game. In Canada, the Prairies and the Maritimes account for the majority of players, according to "Mister 29," Robert Young, a Vancouverite who spent forty years marketing Canada's unique contribution to the game, The 29 Crib Board.

Back in 1956, Young was a manufacturers' rep for leisure novelty items. In the '20s, he'd have been called a "drummer." Always on the lookout for an item on which he could make a margin instead of just a commission, he spotted a homemade board that put the first new twist on the game of Cribbage since Suckling was skunking his tenant farmers in the local pub—a wooden board in the shape of the number 29, the game's rare highest scoring hand, instead of the traditional 'racetrack' board, a sort of compressed and elongated S as old as the Pharaohs

Young tracked down the maker, Edward M. Hirst, a Burnaby truck driver confined to a wheelchair as a result of the polio epidemic of the 1950s. Fatally weakened by polio, Hirst died at thirty-five of pneumonia in 1960, but his widow Vera remarried and still lives in Vancouver.

## Life of a Salesman

"When Eddy first came home from the hospital, he wanted to teach me to play Crib," Vera Spurr recalled when we chatted in March of 2001, "But we didn't have a board. We had to borrow one from next door. Ed said, 'I'll make us a board. What shape should I make it?' I didn't know. I barely knew how to play. I said, 'All I hear is people saying Twenty Nine!' So he carved a board in the shape of that number. People who saw it wanted one, so he started making them to sell. We had children and it was something he could do to make a little income for us. He kept making them right up until he died."

Robert Young paid the Hirsts a royalty, added marketing wrinkles of his own, like the compartment in the back that holds a pack of cards and extra pegs, and beat a path to the world's door with The 29 Crib Board. On his first trip, he pre-sold four hundred units on the Prairies, only to discover the guy who said he could produce them quickly and easily could do neither.

"They screwed up the wood. It was terrible, but your word as a salesman was sacred in those days," Young recalls with Willy Loman-like *angst*. "I said I'd deliver that order if I had to make them myself. We made it, but I must've lost a couple of bucks on each one."

Luckily, he found Henry Zomruiter, a Dutchman who'd worked in a toy factory, who put his whole family to work in his garage workshop and began producing fine boards faster than Young's Ryco Sales could move them.

"He was making two or three hundred a week," Young says. "He had about five thousand of them in his shop and they were selling slowly. I kept giving him money and told him to keep at it." In the 1970s, Young tried to reduce costs by having the boards made in mainland China, but problems of warping and poor craftsmanship that plagued early manufacture re-surfaced. "Out of two thousand units, seven hundred were returned," Young remembers ruefully.

Young tried to sell the board into the obvious market, England, ancestral home of the game, but a hand-crafted item was over the price-point for the working class who made up the bulk of the Cribbage-playing demographic.

"We tried to sell it at trade shows, but it was always just a couple of dollars over the market," Young recalls. He may also have failed to reckon with innate English conservatism, especially where ancient games like cricket and Cribbage are concerned. American customers, on the other hand, still cheerfully send him money orders to cover the cost of multiple boards and courier charges to obtain the ideal gift for a Crib player.

Though he's sold "Eighty or ninety thousand" of the boards over the years, lately, Young admits, sales have slumped and he's a lot older than Arthur Miller's dying salesman. But Young is a drummer to the core with the soul of the kind of salesman Arthur Miller transformed into a modern tragic culture-hero. Once I'd contacted him about writing this article, he not only called me dozens of times to add little remembered details to anecdotes; he also sent me a new Mister 29 deluxe wood crib board with cards and extra pegs.

Contacted for a photo by Jim Sutherland, the editor who published the original version of this piece in the *Vancouver Sun*, Young appeared in the newsroom with a glad hand and gift boards for Jim and others as well. Having sensed a marketing opportunity, he worked us all like a veteran tent evangelist storming out of retirement with a "Come to Jesus" spiel and a steel-toed boot for the Devil's ass. I could hear the mix of astonishment and exasperation in Sutherland's normally understated phone manner when he described Young's invasion of the newsroom.

But there was something more in Sutherland's voice; a kind of exhilaration, a contact high. A real person, not "larger than life," as journalists love to say, but merely "large as life," had penetrated the bureaucracy of bullshit, the temple of faux-facts, to blow a jet of fresh air up their skirts. Robert Young in his salesman's suit, swinging his sample case and rattling out the patter like an antique machine-gun, mowing down ranks of institutionalized reporters and journalism school interns, finishing off the wounded, hand-to-handshake, must have been something to see. I'm chuffed to have played a small part in that massacre.

## Pegging Out

"I don't think Cribbage will ever become extinct," Young told me, "It's too good a game. James Sinclair, former MP and father of Margaret Trudeau, called it the greatest card game for two people ever invented. As for the Mister 29 Crib Board, I've just delivered the last of my current stock to The Games People in Gastown. I don't know if I'm going to have any more made."

If he doesn't, the value of existing 29 Crib boards can only go one way, the way of the handmade crokinole boards you couldn't give away at a garage sale ten years ago. Look for an original 29 board made by the hand of E.M Hirst to turn up on *The Antiques Roadshow* sometime soon. The deluxe hand-machined version currently sells for about $40 from The Games People or similar boutiques. Cheaper versions in plastic lurk around, manufactured by the novelty and playing card giant, Bicycle, who lifted the concept of the 29 Crib Board without paying a dime in royalties to Hirst or Robert Young. Why didn't Young sue the thieving seat off Bicycle?

"I knew they were stealing from us when they brought out that crappy plastic board," Young explained. "But as an independent broker, I depended on Bicycle for a lot of other products I sold. What could I do? If I sued them over the board, they'd stop selling to me and I wouldn't be able to pay my lawyer. They knew that and so did I. There was no point fighting it out."

My new Mister 29 Crib Board is in mint condition. I haven't used it much. Now my Mom is playing four-handed Crib with the Father, Son, and Holy Ghost, my sister has our old one, veteran of innumerable family Crib tournaments that went on long past everyone's bedtime. She also has the Edward M. Hirst Memorial Cup—a stained, cracked teacup my brother Bill used to hold over his head and dance around the house after final victory like an NHL hockey captain with the Stanley Cup, proclaiming it, "Symblematic of Crib-playing supremacy!" to the neighbourhood at 3 a.m. Symblematic? It's a perfectly cromulent word.

## The Cribbage Bitch

I still can't play Crib without thinking of my Nan. By the time I was fourteen, I loathed her, and Cribbage embodied my rage. The game revealed the contradictory aspects of her conflicted personality; the kindly Grandmother who would spend endless hours patiently teaching children to play a complex card game, and the Bitch who would proceed to ruthlessly beat them at it, then gloat more savagely than any schoolyard bully.

Born at the turn of the last century on the Isle of Wight, within her living memory the Wright Brothers made their first powered flight and men landed on the moon. People of her generation suffered the most traumatic effects of "future shock," the escalating pace of change Alvin Toffler made the theme of his Seventies best-seller. Many of them suffered from hardening of the attitudes in later life, the mind's defence against the onslaught of too much new information, an overdose of change.

Her father was a Regimental Sergeant-Major, a career non-commissioned officer in the days when soldiers' wives received no allotment from the British Army. Army wives raised families on whatever they could sift from the pockets of husbands after publicans and whores had relieved them of the bulk of their meagre pay. Handsome, with impressive whiskers and moustache, Violet's father was a brutal drunkard and whoremaster who returned home only to perform one conjugal duty: the regular beating and sexual subjugation of his wife. Understandably, Violet did not grow up with a high opinion of men.

She nursed and later married a soft-hearted Lancastrian who survived WWI by killing Germans at Vimy and Passchendale, but who couldn't set a mouse-trap because a mouse once saved him from a sniper's bullet in the trenches. When he returned to Canada, she went with him. When Bill was lucky enough to find work, he often gave away most of his pay packet to unemployed men who told him hard luck stories on his way home. Because he was such a soft touch, Violet became harder in order to protect her brood of six children, two of whom died in infancy, one horrifically, from meningitis.

By the time I knew her, in the smug prosperous post-war 1950s, she'd survived two world wars, the Depression, the deaths of two children and the eccentricities of a chronically improvident mate. When Grandad was a boy, his blind father owned a pub and did well despite his handicap. One day the pub caught fire. Ten-year-old Billy ran into the blazing building to rescue the family fortune. A mere boy, money to him meant *coin*, so at the risk of his life he salvaged a bag of pennies and left the paper notes to burn. The script of his life was written in that early act of futile heroism.

## She Who Must Be Obeyed

After my Dad died, Nan and Grandad moved in with us for a while to help my mother. Lots of Generation X people have had the experience of moving back to their parents' house and their Boomer parents have had *their* aged parents move in with them. While we'd love to believe the Asian model of the extended multi-generational family is the right one, in our culture it's a pressure cooker that stresses the notion of "family" to its limits.

Nan assumed the role of Matriarch of the household. She infantilized my mother and manipulated me and my brothers and sister by emotional bullying as ruthless as her Crib playing, rewarding obedience with affectionate spoiling and rebellion with merciless sarcastic persecution. If you called her bluff when she made cutting remarks about your clothes, hair, or friends, she played the Grandmother Card and burst into tears of misunderstood altruism.

It was like being trapped in the Actors Studio with Bea Arthur on crystal meth. I said as much in the course of our final over-the-top-rope Battle Royal when I was fifteen. When I confronted her about the way she manipulated the family, she threw a teary fit and tried to drive away in the middle of the night. While my mother attempted to talk her back into the house, I laughed and told her to go sleep in the park. She and Grandad moved out shortly after. I missed playing Crib against her, but that was all.

I hardly spoke to her for twenty years, even when Grandad died. In her nineties, we were seated together at some big family bun-fight and she played the Frail Old Lady role for all it was worth. Though she was about as frail as an M1 tank, she whined, "I never get to sit beside my eldest Grandson anymore," as if her other twelve grandchildren hardly counted. I wasn't even the eldest—my cousins Bill and Linda are older by a couple of years, but this kind of convenient confusion is a talent of senile delinquents that she possessed in abundance.

"Whose fault is that?" I snapped, as if our final donnybrook had occurred the night before. The thing I could never forgive was her willingness, despite being a very strong woman, to use the appearance of frailty to torment her own family. We hadn't played Crib since that fateful night and for a moment I was tempted to ask her if she wanted to get out the cards and play a rubber or two, just to see if I could settle my account with her once and for all.

I didn't. We were too much alike to reconcile, heirs of the genetic legacy of adverse personality traits we shared. She spent her last years in the lock-down at Riverview Hospital, a victim of multiple cross-medication mistakes that turned her into a violent psychotic. She tried to make life hell for the staff, but they were strangers, people she couldn't reduce to tears with a few cruel words. Like a witch deprived of her talismans, personal bits of hair, skin, or fingernails to seal her charms, she was powerless.

In the end she was a casualty of time and history—a woman who, if she couldn't have things her way, wouldn't have them at all—an attitude I learned and still struggle to overcome, thanks to her unfortunate example. She died in her late nineties, demented, but unbeaten at Crib.

## Like to Love Thee More

It's occurred to me that if I had visited her in the lock-down, played Crib with her every week, it might have given her a way to return from the dementia into which she retreated. Suppose a few rubbers of Crib against me had brought her back to reality. Would that have been an act of kindness? She'd have been the last to thank me. It would never have occurred to her to thank me for anything unless she thought it would make it easier to get me to do something else she had in mind.

I'm grateful to her for many things. She taught me about people, their ability to say one thing, then act in a manner completely contrary to what they've said and delude even themselves with the most convoluted rationalizations when the contradiction is challenged. For a nascent writer, she was an all-you-can-eat smorgasbord in the emotional famine of Eisenhower-era suburbia. With all her flaws, she was someone who'd lived as hard as life itself, like Robert Young.

As I grew up, I lost a lot of money at a penny a point, double for skunks, to old sailors I crewed with on a yacht based in Coal Harbour, men who'd bumped around the world in British, American, Dutch, and Norwegian merchant marines enough times to make Magellan dizzy. The old salts played Crib like my Nan, for blood and money. They gave no quarter, cut no slack and called Muggins on every miscounted hand.

Karl "Charlie" Johansen had lived in fo'c'sles since he was a fourteen-year-old cabin boy on a Norwegian whaler that ran under canvas. He developed leukaemia in his eighties and beat it for fifteen years. He also beat me at Crib with the same casual, thorough brutality as my Nan. I never whined because if I did, he wouldn't play me anymore and I wouldn't get to hear his stories as he pegged points off any card I put down, somehow making as much out of bad hands as I did when I got the cut and had a "mitt-full."

In time, I understood that my grandmother had taught me more than a card game. She taught me to lose without losing my temper, just shuffle the cards and play the rubber. Like all great card games, Cribbage doesn't only teach arithmetic or how to estimate the element of chance as a percentage. It teaches what might be called "character," a philosophy of life, expressed by Sir John Suckling:

*"Out upon it I have loved*
*Three whole days together;*
*And am like to love thee more,*
*If it prove fair weather."*

And if it rains, my darling, we'll stay in and play Crib.

# FIFTEEN

# Last Resort

Exiting Whistler's then-new Brewhouse a few years ago, I ambled out a different door than I'd entered and into a paranoid nightmare. In the fading evening light, I blundered through some immaculately Dutch-paved galleries and courtyards before realizing I was lost. If I'd had soap-opera amnesia I'd still have known I was in Whistler from all the sweatshirt logos in shop windows. I just didn't know where in Whistler, or which direction led back to my car. Anywhere on the Village Stroll in the original townsite, I'd have trusted gravity and my liver's compass to lead me to Tapley's Pub. But Whistler had sprouted a joined-at-the-overpass conjoined twin on the northwest side of Village Gate Boulevard, and I was on the unfamiliar side of town.

Yet it was all too familiar. Not in the comforting sense, but with the disconcerting edginess of a deja-vu experience or anxiety dream. Buildings hemming the maze looked exactly like those in the original town, a kind of generic Swiss-Tyrolean set Ralph Lauren would concoct for an après-skiwear ad. Asymmetrical walks designed to provide non-threatening novelty and casual delight to daytime strollers appeared surreally warped and deserted, as vaguely sinister as a Giorgio De Chirico painting.

In the 1960s British television series, *The Prisoner*, a rogue secret agent is drugged and imprisoned in The Village, a themed seaside community whose twee design seems inspired by Noddy books and Beatrix Potter illustrations. Escapees are pursued along the beach and smothered by huge animated balloons that resemble giant condoms. The machinery of repression is run by a changing cast, all of whom call themselves Number Two and inform the agent, played by Patrick McGoohan, "I am Number Two. You are Number Six."

McGoohan's signature line, "I am not a number! I am a free man!" was in the boarding lounge of my Scream Express when a guy wandered into the square and kindly led me out of the labyrinth. In a parking lot filled with acres of nearly identical cars, I immediately knew where to find mine. No giant condom pursued me, but I looked over my shoulder until I was well out of town.

In the November 12, 2004, issue of Whistler's *Pique Newsmagazine*, editor Bob Barnett reported on a meeting of Tourism Whistler members as they opened a black-bordered telegram: the results of a visitor survey conducted over the previous year. It was meant to explain what nervous local gossip had already established: Two consecutive years of falling visitor numbers, empty rooms, and continuing high overheads had resulted in business failures, with some merchants pulling out of the Village instead of fighting to get in. A whopping thirty-five percent of visitors surveyed said they would not come back to Whistler because it is too expensive. The Ski Club of Great Britain complained that prices in Whistler were ridiculously high. American visits had dropped by more than sixteen percent. A lack of family-friendly activities came up, as did poor front desk service due to multiple property managers involved in time-share condo bookings.

## RAINCITY: VANCOUVER REFLECTIONS

In a qualifying heat for the Gold Medal for Understatement, Diana Lyons of the Delta Village Suites commented that Whistler "doesn't Google well" with keywords like "budget," "moderate," and "affordable." Resort operators know people spend more freely on holidays than they do at home, but they are at home when they check their VISA bills and find they paid more than $12 for a cheeseburger. And people who have money *do* check their bills closely, knowing that every two-bit pimp with a junior college marketing degree sees them as cash cows to be milked.

"Some of the issue is as much about perception as reality, but in tourism as in politics, perception often is reality," Barnett observed astutely. Strolling through the expensively crafted lodge ambiance of the expanded Village, the monotonous repetition of bar, bistro, boutique and gift shop creates an impression not unlike downtown Reno, notorious for placing Keno boards even above urinals. The notion that Whistler is nothing more than an outdoor mall designed to make you walk past as many retailers as possible in the process of getting anywhere, aiming to relieve you of large amounts of your disposable income along the way, is inescapable.

Barnett's observation about perception cuts deeper than predictable gripes about high prices and indifferent service. Whistler is so artificially contrived to make money that it actually sends a visual message at odds with its purpose. Lots of nice people live in Whistler. It has one of the most active and talented writers' groups in the province. But the public face of the place is the Village and it provokes mixed reactions in many visitors; not just because it seems determined to remind you that you can't really afford—thus don't deserve—to be there, but also because it's so conspicuously not a real town. If Whistler can't resolve this fundamental perceptual ambivalence, the 2010 Olympics could be the event that turns it into a ghost-condo complex as sad as the many B.C. mining bonanza towns that were briefly the biggest and richest cities north of Chicago or San Francisco.

In the 1960s, the village in *The Prisoner*, (an actual resort in Wales), was on the cutting edge of resort architecture, which has been around as a distinct genre since Roman Emperors built luxurious getaway villas on the isle of Capri. Previously, wealthy Romans had maintained comfortable agricultural estates, to which they retired in summer to play at farming and commune with their redneck roots. The imperial fad for seaside villas caused many to fatally opt for the balmy charms of Pompeii and Herculaneum—the West Palm Beaches of their time, where volcanoes instead of hurricanes were apt to suddenly depress property values. Resort architecture has always been a whore to great wealth; witness the Long Island mansions ludicrously described as summerhouses by New York social register types in the early 1900s.

Amusement parks like Brighton Pier, Coney Island midway, Disneyland/DisneyWorld, and Las Vegas' themed casinos, are carnival imitations of the grand casinos and spas of Europe's imperial 19th century. Their overblown glitter is meant to dazzle the working and middle classes, but at least they're *inclusive*. Since ancient Roman times, the consistent characteristic of resort architecture has been the ironically expensive fabrication, not of grandeur, but of an idealized, simpler, more authentic lifestyle. So while most of us gasp at the current million-plus and multi-million dollar prices of a cabin in the woods in Whistler, our shock is either naïve or faked as a first-date orgasm. Despite its pretensions to simplicity, resort architecture remains fundamentally elitist and exclusionist.

Nineteenth century Norwegian immigrants brought the winter pastime of sliding down snowy slopes on wooden slats to North America, which had plenty of mountains and nothing else to do with them, yet skiing only became fashionable here in the 1950s. Wooden skis with non-release suicide bindings, rope tows and T-bar lifts required dedication that made the sport a hard sell. Anyone who has experienced the invigorating effects of hypothermia, frostbite, windburn, and glare-blindness knows that it has never really been about skiing. It's about lounging in loud sweaters and tight pants around rock fireplaces in rustic lodges, nibbling snacks whose main ingredient is melted cheese, sipping coffee drinks spiked with pungent liqueurs, and the delicious friction of snow-tanned flesh under feather quilts. Once the American royalty of Hollywood stars like Gary Cooper were photographed frolicking on Aspen and Sun Valley slopes in unattractive woollen clothing, the future of skiing—and ski resorts—was assured.

By the early '70s, pseudo-sophisticates summed up this lifestyle with the borrowed French phrase, *après*-ski, or, more pretentiously, just *après*. People were seriously using it apropos of Whistler when the future townsite was an open pit garbage buffet for bears, the only bar was the grotty Ski Boot pub, and most residents lived at Whistler Creek lift-base in a squatters' camp of old trailers connected by tarps known as The Ghetto, whose pretyphoid ambiance had a long mogul-row to hoe before Gstaad or St. Moritz would feel threatened. It took thirty years, but the faith of early visionaries like Franz Wilhelmsen was vindicated in 2001, when Vancouver beat out venerable Salzburg's bid for the 2010 Winter Games.

In the late '60s, pioneer promoters may have been a tad naïve to think that treating an IOC scout to pitchers of draft at the Boot and some leg-wrestling with a twenty-two-year-old ex-Laurentian ski bunny in the back of a rusty VW van would clinch an Olympic bid. Hobbled by a total lack of site infrastructure and by 130 kilometres of road that looked like it had been laid out by an Irish surveyor on his way home from the pub, they enlisted the star quality of Canadian Olympic ski champion Nancy Greene and coach/husband Al Raine to get the attention of the provincial government.

In 1975, the Resort Municipality of Whistler was created to market the snow and *après* for all they were worth. A cabal of local celebrities and real estate shills formed one of the first councils and disgraced itself by spending more money than it collected from taxes and speculative land sales, an act of fiscal nonchalance punishable by criminal charges under the Municipal Act. The province made a controversial decision to bail out the bankrupt municipality at B.C. taxpayers' expense and replace the councillors with ones who could add and subtract from something bigger than a bar tab.

Having twigged that being *Burgermeisters* is only fun if you have an actual *Burg* to *meister*, succeeding councils acquired a "town" to forestall IOC quibbling that there wasn't anything at Whistler but mountains. To the ongoing discomfiture of the local bruin population, a Village of Whistler was rapidly erected on the site of the former garbage dump. When existing but distressed working towns are gentrified into resorts, some elements of authenticity are preserved at grid-level and through restoration, as in many Swiss and Tyrolean farming hamlets and former Western American mining towns that have become skiing destinations. Whistler's instant alpine village looked like something pre-fabbed by schnapps-maddened elves in the IKEA Hall of the Mountain King, flat-shipped for assembly, marked ONE CLOCK TOWER, TEN RUSTIC INNS, ONE DOZEN QUAINT SHOPS. INSERT TABS A INTO SLOTS B.

The German word *gemutlich* is often translated as "cosy." It describes a home, restaurant or inn whose occupants are congenial, as well as a style of bourgeois décor that may be rustic, but not rough. In Swiss and Bavarian villages, it's a by-product of long occupation by people who indulge their artistic side in the ornamentation of the practical. Faked, it means lots of non-structural laminate beams, cultured stone cladding, cowbells and cuckoo clocks and rosmaling on non-functional shutters until you could hork up your *Sachertorte*. The Germans also have a word for this: *kitsch*. Hitler loved this shit. Top Nazis had a whole compound in the mountains above Berchtesgaden done up in ersatz-alpen style, where they could drag up in *loden* and *lederhosen* with their dirndl-skirted consorts and pretend to be heroic woodcutters from Grimm's fairy tales instead of the big bad wolves they were.

Like other ski resorts, Whistler bought into the ersatz-alpen design concept. One of the inherent kinks of resort architecture is the perceived need to maintain a thematic fantasy, which discourages experimentation and evolution in the built environment. In Whistler, maintaining the dubious integrity of the monotonous international "alpine" design theme is the job of municipal planners and the Advisory Planning Commission made up of volunteers from the community. Officially, their mission is to work with developers to facilitate the adoption of building designs and facades that will meet with the approval of council and result in the swift granting of permits...blah, blah. In fact, they're the *Alpengeist* Gestapo whose agenda is to prevent pop-stars and other vulgar rich thugs from building pink Parthenon-inspired stucco villas, or Trumpish developers from erecting garish hotels with inappropriate Taj Mahal or Chinese pagoda themes. They're backed up by toothy bylaws that even regulate signage, especially the neon signatures of national and transnational retail and fast food chains, most of whom have been successfully prevented from lowering Whistler's perceived tone.

Whistler's insistence on controlling building height, appearance and signage is not necessarily a bad thing. Would to God more B.C. municipalities exercised their legitimate right to decide how their towns look. Halfway to Whistler, the traditional business district of Squamish has been gutted by highway-to-hell strip malls, where companies have been allowed to drop characterless corporate units onto highly visible sites with hardly a squeak of protest from local politicians for fear of annulling the supposed mystic marriage of investment and jobs. While Squamish wags its tail in the air to show that it's any-corporate-body's bitch, Whistler growls like a chained St. Bernard that has slurped its brandy cask and is ready to chew the legs off anybody not in designer ski-wear.

The business end of that chain is held by Intrawest. Anytime there's a pissing contest in Whistler, Intrawest makes the biggest yellow hole in the snow. Originally an urban real estate development company, in 1986 Intrawest bought the Blackcomb Mountain operation and married it to Whistler operations shortly thereafter. Recognizing that the resort industry is a jackpot fattened by Baby Boomers—the wealthiest and most numerous generation of North American consumers—in 1994 the company shucked its urban interests to concentrate on acquiring and marketing upscale resort properties, especially ski resorts. In a mere decade, Intrawest has bought or become the major player in the dozen most prominent ski resorts in North America, as well as entering into partnerships with several established European ski resorts. By its own admission, a cornerstone of Intrawest's policy is the pseudo-quaint alpine-themed "pedestrian village" meant to "enhance the resort experience"—and maximize the extraction of visitor dollars off the slopes as well as on.

Intrawest's genius is that it knew from the get-go it wasn't in the ski-lift racket; it was in the fully packaged lifestyle-resort business. One of the cardinal rules of industry is never to let the mill be idle. Accordingly, Intrawest has systematically transformed its alpine resorts into year-round destinations, integrating golf, eco, and adventure tourism—anything that will keep its Club Intrawest hotel rooms and high-end private condos booked. This diversified, all-season marketing plan also cannily recognizes that Boomers who made *aprés* a marketable commodity aren't going to bust moguls or deep powder on Zimmer-frame skis. Around 2010, year of the Big Olympic Bonus, Boomers who built the business will start hanging up their slats and turning to low-impact activities, where the chances of simultaneously catching pneumonia and breaking a hip are slimmer.

Like the smaller retailers and restaurants, Intrawest and the big hotel chains that are heavily invested in Whistler depend upon the minimum wage krill who cling to the bottom links of the resort food chain for tips or the perk of a season ski pass. These are the people who interact with visitors face-to-face, making or breaking the bubble blown by the resort architects. In the wake of the Tourism Whistler survey, staff all over Whistler are no doubt undergoing compulsory, inquisitional service-motivation seminars—middle managers' instinctive ass-covering response to negative client input. But it's delusional to blame staff for Whistler's service failures, at any level. These people work in a town that makes it very clear their presence is tolerated only because somebody has to serve and clean up after *le grande luxe*.

As a thirty-year observer of Whistler politics, I've watched several councils elected, each promising to address the issue of affordable staff housing—housing that doesn't involve sharing with sixteen other people and sleeping in shifts while the off-shift parties on around you. Despite the municipality's 300-odd acres of assorted Crown land, basically given to the resort over the years to provide employee housing, every proposed staff housing initiative has floundered because absentee millionaires petition council in aggrieved tones, protesting that they're in favour of staff housing, just Not In My Back Yard. They raise the dread spectre of multimillion-dollar equity eroded by proximity to ghetto dorms infested with inebriated Aussie lift-workers, likely to stage pick-up-a-longneck-with-your-asshole contests within sight or hearing of their sybaritic chalets and cedar-decked hot tubs.

At the bottom of the same page as Barnett's November 12 *Pique* editorial, a real estate ad offered "Whistler's Best Priced Single Family Home"; a vaguely Swiss, three-bedroom plus loft, with a one-bedroom suite rentable to half a dozen shifties, priced at $765,000. In the real world at the time, current house price stats indicated that you could buy an average house in Vancouver *and* one in Toronto for that stake. Once again, the perception is that people who own Whistler would prefer that people who work there would simply get out of town when not required to carry ski bags, pour shooters, bus tables, or mop up the vomited excess of living large. In fantasy WhistlerWorld, workers live in Squamish or Pemberton—never mind that for people making minimum wage, having to buy, insure, and fuel a beater to drive thirty to forty kilometres to work every day is a financial burden proportionally more punitive than lease payments on a new Ford Expedition.

Whistler crows because its annual cattle-call, the fall Job Fair, attracted line-ups this year—in contrast to a couple of previous seasons where help was hard to get for the first time in decades. Whoopee is premature, since incoming staff will quickly become as cynical and demoralized as veterans by the economic realities of serving in Heaven. Working for a ski pass, most will join the underclass of a deeply polarized community, working weekends when tours and rich owners clog the slopes and skiing or boarding weekdays when they have the snow mostly to themselves. Ironically, the people who make the greatest use of what is supposed to be the community's primary asset are the workers who can't really afford to live there.

The future of Whistler as a community ultimately depends on people who work and live there, but a thirty percent jump in real estate values in the Sea to Sky corridor following the acceptance of Vancouver's 2010 Olympic bid made home ownership problematic for non-transient working people. Last year, building lots went on sale in Britannia Beach, ten kilometres south of Squamish, for just under $200,000.00 and sold out in twenty-four hours, despite the toxic legacy of the giant abandoned copper mine. From Lions Bay to Squamish, the mephitic stench of pulp mills has been replaced by the smell of greed. Prices in Pemberton have gone ballistic and in Whistler itself, that three-quarters of a million tag for a single family resort property actually looks like a bargain.

The dogs in the manger started snarling over the "legacies" of an Olympics that was six years away. In Vancouver, venues were relocated, pitting one metro municipality against another. Squamish is squealing about being pushed off the teat because the official Vancouver Olympic Committee threatened legal action over the town's "Heart of 2010" slogan, not to mention a local contractor's use of the name "Olympic Valley," and a local woman's sale of a related internet domain name to German pornographers. In the November 18 *Pique*, Whistler filed final notice of an application to extend its municipal boundaries south to Brandywine Provincial Park—a move to establish a thick bulwark against carnie hustlers who might otherwise erect tacky mini-golf courses or reptile ranches on the resort's doorstep. The biggest legacy of all—multimillion dollar improvements to the Sea to Sky Highway—was well on the way to giving all B.C. taxpayers grief in a place that may still be sore from the original Whistler bailout.

While Tourism Whistler members conduct staff purges and the Resort Municipality annexes additional *Lebensraum* to buffer the illusion of WhistlerWorld, solutions to the fundamental problem of Whistler's perceived lack of authenticity as a community are belatedly being sought. Over budget and overdue, Volume One of the *Comprehensive Sustainability Plan*, a forty-two page paper that took three years to write, was adopted by the municipality in December and grandly renamed *Whistler 2020—Moving to a Sustainable Future*. Wrapping itself in the sustainability flag is a smart PR move, as is the municipality's adoption of LEED (Leadership in Energy and Environmental Design) standards for public buildings. In December, Whistler received its first LEED certificate in recognition of the green building practices used in the Spring Creek Fire Hall. Alas, real 20-20 vision also sees people building chalets that use multiple old growth cedar trunks as decorative columns to support huge decks and verandas—a design flourish that sends a decidedly different environmental message.

One thing the CSP got right was to kibosh the idea of a separate residential community seventeen kilometres south in the Callaghan Valley, once touted as a possible Olympic athlete's village and future employee housing site—an option that would create a de facto 'workers' ghetto' excluded from the community.

The other hopeful glimmer is the municipality's eleventh hour hire of Whistler Housing Authority veteran Steve Bayly as a housing expediter. Bayly has been given a scant year to cure a rash that has been chafing Whistler's crotch for a decade. When his contract ends, he'll have to take up bomb disposal or test-driving Ferraris to relax after a stint of trying to balance the interests of workers, corporate stakeholders, and NIMBY millionaires.

Bayly has one ace in his fanny pack. He was involved in the original design of Whistler's business/industrial park, Function Junction, at the present main entrance to the municipality, six kilometres south of the Village. Just off Highway 99 and screened by firs, it's basically a long street flanked by rectangular pre-engineered buildings whose design is industrial or at least primarily functional. No glue-lam beams or mock rock. Visually, the effect is reminiscent of Main Street in an Old West film set, but there are hardware stores, a car dealership, the relaxed Millar Creek Café, even a barbershop. All Function Junction lacks is a local grocery/pharmacy General Store and a pub to become the nucleus of a real community.

Hemmed by escarpments to the west and the Millar Creek wetlands to the northwest, Function Junction has one logical way to expand. Instead of chipping away at Garibaldi Provincial Park to extend ski areas fewer people are going to use in coming decades,

Whistler could co-opt the Interpretive Forest directly across the highway from Function Junction as the site for affordable staff housing and the resident working population. A basic road network already exists and the land is mostly flat (by B.C. standards), all the way to the backyard park of Cheakamus Lake. Permanent and transient working people would have a community tastefully screened from the highway to avoid offending the sensibilities of visiting millionaires, with a real town centre within walking distance. Whistler Transit already runs buses between Function Junction and the official Village. It's a minimum effort, no-brainer, win-win solution that could create an organically viable, authentic town and, in the long run, *that* would be an Olympic legacy worth having.

## Postscript

It might have been. By 2017, some housing had been built across the highway from Function Junction and the industrial park was being expanded, but the ongoing housing crisis in Whistler was, predictably, worse, not better. Skyrocketing property values in Pemberton and Squamish, as these towns filled up with Whistler wannabes from Vancouver, made both towns as unaffordable to their own working class as Whistler. Ironically, the lowest paid members of Whistler's work force—usually young and single— have the best chance of getting a roof over their heads, as long as they can stand the party-dorm ambiance of staff housing apartments. Despite twenty years of effort by the Whistler Housing Authority, it is the people trying to raise families in the town, often well-paid professionals like healthcare workers, police officers, municipal employees, and teachers, who are falling through the cracks. Disqualified from dorm housing and unable to afford even the smallest stratospherically priced properties, most of them live out of town and commute. These professions embody the core values of the culture at large in small communities where they work and *live*. If they can't afford to live in the community where they work for eight or twelve hours, that turns them into mercenaries. It also means the community they serve is losing half to two-thirds of the moral added-value of their presence as citizens. That's a devil's bargain no community with a future can afford to make.

SIXTEEN

\*! (boom)

October 20, 2014; eleven days before Halloween.

A man who blew up a homemade pipe bomb in his own face in Vancouver's Olympic Village early Monday morning won't tell police why or how he made the explosive device. Around 1:00 a.m. paramedics called police after they tended to a man at Columbia Street and West 1st Avenue and he admitted that the massive cut to his face was from a bomb, according to Sgt. Randy Fincham of the Vancouver Police Department.

The man, who is "well known to police," was sent to hospital with "significant non-life-threatening" injuries, Fincham said. Fincham said police are still investigating the incident, but haven't recommended charges because the officers would need to prove criminal intent, and "couldn't find where this thing was built or where it was lit off."

"Sometimes making poor choices in life isn't criminal," Fincham said. (o.canada.com)

## Pulp Fiction remix:

@20 seconds: *Sometimes, making poor choices in life isn't criminal.* In fact, Canada's Explosives Act (1985), is unequivocal: nobody is allowed to "make or manufacture any explosive, wholly or in part, except in a licensed factory." In this case, the evidence of illegal manufacture was blown up, but making a pipe bomb is, nevertheless, a criminal act.

@8 seconds: Though "known to police," this bombster apparently isn't ganged-up or politically motivated. He's a loner and what cops and medical staff call a *frequent flyer*; the kind of whack-job who spends lots of time in emergency rooms and custody cells because of his proclivity for "making bad choices in life" and whose pre-sentencing reports are full of phrases like "insufficiently developed mechanisms for impulse control."

@15 seconds: VPD officers "couldn't find where this thing was built or where it was set off." Depending on the amount and strength of the explosive, damage could be confined to one room, especially in a concrete basement. Pipe shrapnel would mangle soft furnishings; to human beings it might be fatal. The sound would be muffled, but neighbours would know it wasn't generated by late night home renovations. No one called police to report the explosion. Would *you* call the cops if your neighbour is the kind of guy who makes bombs?

It's been a while since I've ducked on an evening walk or jolted out of my chair at the window-rattling *ka-boom* of a pipe bomb. For a few years after moving to Squamish in the early 1990s I'd still hear one or two unmistakable detonations splinter the crisp autumn air around Halloween. It's a sound I know well. I grew up in North Vancouver.

October, 1966; one week before Halloween:

The garage belongs to Swede Johnson's father. It is attached to a house in a quiet residential street near Edgemont Village, three blocks of retail in the middle of a North Vancouver suburb called Capilano Highlands. I am sixteen, present only because Howie Harrigan has been letting me hang out with him as a sort of mascot and sorcerer's apprentice. Howie is almost nineteen. His fists and boots have put the North Van brand on guys from as far away as South Burnaby and New West. He is known in certain circles all over Vancouver as a guy not to be fucked with.

In imitation of Howie's, my hair is sculpted into a duck-tail and brow waterfall by half a pound of Brylcreem. Like him, I wear black pointed boots with Spanish heels, drainpipe black jeans and a white t-shirt, but with a plain denim jean-jacket that marks me as a squire, not a knight of the black leather.

A few older guys give the hard eye when they see a junior high punk, but Howie's thighs in skin-tight jeans look like he's wearing football pads underneath. He is famous for having caved in a car door with one kick when some letter-sweater boys inside lipped him off in the parking lot of King's Burgers on Marine Drive. Then he grabbed the buckled door, tore it off its hinges, skimmed it across the lot and told them to fuck off. They did. Transported in a back seat up to the Highlands Pool Hall, the door was propped on a chair and venerated like a trophy of the heroic age.

Swede Johnson is eighteen, still in Grade 10 on the Industrial

Arts program. He only stays in school so he can have access to the shop and tools to work on the '57 Chevy he races at Mission dragstrip all summer. In the rainy season, the car reposes in this garage, having its blower-supercharged 327 cubic-inch mill souped-up by amateur alchemists. Blood red, its hindquarters raised threateningly on massive slicks, the car hunches on the concrete pad like a predatory beast in its lair. The low front grille is black and empty as a man-eating mouth.

Under an Elvis helmet of gleaming blond locks, Swede is a restless demiurge, Caliban in greasy blue coveralls. When not fully occupied with hot-rod necromancy, he applies his skills to small shit like the manufacture of zip guns; single-shot homemade firearms capable of firing a .45 caliber bullet or .410 shot shell. Every Halloween, he sets off a pipe bomb louder than anything anyone on the North Shore will hear for a year.

If you're lucky, a pipe bomb is something you might hear but never see. This year, thanks to Howie, there's a chance I will actually see Swede's pipe bomb before it becomes legendary.

On the first school day after Halloween, the question, whispered or scribbled on notes passed in class, "Did you *hear* it?" pervaded our school's halls and classrooms. If you were grounded on Halloween, you opened your bedroom window wide as it would go and sat there, tense as a cat, so you could say you'd heard Swedes' pipe bomb and it was the biggest, scariest fucking sound you'd ever heard, when anyone asked. Even up near the treeline, where

I lived, you could hear the thunder of pure mindless menace unleashed.

A pipe bomb produces a rent in the atmosphere you can feel a mile away on a clear night and hear a lot farther, a deep shock-and-awesome bass chord whose aftermath is uncanny, almost reverent silence. On Halloween, a pipe bomb exploding mutes all the snaps, bangs and whizzes of mere fireworks the way the long ululating howl of a lone wolf silences a pack of yipping coyotes. After it, the loudest cherry bomb in your fireworks bag seems no more than a squeak, hardly worth a match.

By the time I was twelve I knew how pipe bombs were made. As Halloween loomed, boys hissed secret formulae into each other's quivering ears like spies, in the washroom at school, in basement rumpus rooms, at the paper shack, at Cadet parades. We spent our 'fireworks allowance' not on Roman Candles and Flaming Fountains but on strings of Ladyfingers, Cherry Bombs, Atom Crackers and Buffalo Bombs.

We didn't set them off egregiously. We scotch-taped them to balsa gliders launched from decks and high windows or inserted them in plastic models of warplanes, battleships, and custom cars we'd painstakingly assembled. Our fathers, who spent evenings helping us build those models, bonding with us in the headachy euphoria of glue, later stood over shards of scorched plastic in the back yard like mourners, shaking their heads, bereft and uncomprehending.

We mined Lincoln Log homes and dollhouses manned by suicide squads of toy soldiers. We blew up expensive educational models of *The Visible Man*, scattering his multi-coloured plastic viscera across the lawn. Our load-out was enhanced with ingredients cribbed from another popular 'educational' toy for boys at the time: the chemistry set. My friend Laurie Preston got one when we were ten. First thing we did was try to make invisible ink. It exploded all over his basement, nearly blinded us, spattered the family laundry and proved to be indelible. Scientific 'discoveries' often result from experiments that produce unanticipated results, so I'm told.

Tooled-up with gunpowder and chemicals, we razed constructions of Tinkertoy and Meccano and reduced innocent farm and zoo play sets to sizzling goo. Imagining ourselves Resistance Fighters, we sabotaged electric trains, even HO layouts on which fathers or older brothers lavished money and obsessive care. We blew up half-full paint cans, causing huge messes in garages, and immolated the Barbie dolls and treasured stuffed animals of younger siblings, triggering childhood emotional traumas.

We caught sixteen kinds of hell from our parents. It didn't stop us. To boys, explosions are as mysteriously and compulsively thrilling as ejaculations. But no matter how creatively we linked the fuses of firecrackers, no matter how inventive or taboo our destructions, they were farts in a high wind compared to a pipe bomb. We all knew how to make one, but none of my friends or I ever pooled our fireworks gunpowder and tried.

## e.g.

Every year in late October and early November the *Vancouver Sun* and *The Province* featured stories about hideous explosive accidents. Invariably these involved boys who'd had fingers blown off or been blinded in one eye due to improper handling of fireworks, (see above), or had been horribly burned *below the waist* when a string of Ladyfingers carelessly dangling from a jeans pocket caught a spark. We all involuntarily crossed our legs when we read about *that*.

Among them, there were always a few accounts of major maiming and disfigurement; (see *massive cut to the face* above), losses of hands or whole arms, total blinding, brain damage and even death due to premature detonations of pipe bombs. We didn't know why a lot of these things seemed to go off on basement workbenches. We only knew they did.

In theory, making a pipe bomb is light work. Google how to and you'll find as many recipes as you would on a visit to foodnetwork.com. You'll also get better information than we got through the Boys' washroom grapevine. Some of it explains why so many pipe bombs assembled in my demolition days went tragically wrong.

e.g.: popular wisdom then said gunpowder in the pipe should be tamped down with a dowel or broom-handle, like the ramrod used to compress powder, ball and wad in old-fashioned muskets. But modern gunpowder acquired, say, by using pliers to pull bullets out of your Dad's hunting ammo and adding the cartridge contents to your stash, is more volatile than the slow-burning stuff musketeers used. Just causing particles of it to rub together under pressure can generate a tiny spark sufficient to ignite the lot. Same goes for threading caps on a loaded pipe. Threads should be swabbed with Vaseline to remove any traces. Crushing a few stray grains as you thread on that second cap after filling the pipe is enough to initiate the devastating consequences noted above.

No one can say Google isn't making us smarter, but serious consideration of the ethical and social questions raised by making this kind of information available to any fuckwit who can read type and has internet access would require publication in volumes.

# terror = terror

"The product of terror is terror," Lenin said. He meant, *the product of terrorism is terror*, but nobody has put it better than the Boss Bolshevik, grand theorist of a miniscule communist splinter-party that used terror to gain control of and dominate the largest nation on earth. For more than four hundred years the homemade bomb has been the duty sidearm of the political revolutionary—and counter-revolutionary.

Persecuted Catholic nobles, including one Guy Fawkes, for whom Britain's annual Festival of Explosives is named, tried to blow up Parliament in the Gunpowder Plot of 1605. In 1800, Royalist contras just missed assassinating Napoleon on his way to the opera with an "infernal machine": a fused wagon-load of barrelled gunpowder touched off by a flintlock pistol whose trigger was pulled by a string. Pre-Revolution Czarist noblemen and ministers were fragged by homemade bombs tossed into their carriages. Where firearms are strictly regulated, as they are by every totalitarian regime, the Improvised Explosive Device, (IED), is the default weapon of the disenfranchised.

A pipe bomb is a homemade grenade, an explosive device almost as dangerous to its user as to its target. In 18th century Europe, tall soldiers were put in special *grenadier* companies. They got bigger hats and extra pay. They also got to carry satchels filled with grenades as primitive and unstable as pipe bombs. Maybe it was assumed that, being tall, they could throw farther—a useful skill when dealing with explosives. Grenadiers were not bombers; they were the delivery system.

Pipe bombs are not military ordinance. No matter how many people are involved in a plot or what cause is espoused to justify their use, pipe bombs are clandestine terror weapons created by solitary specialists, meant to be set off when and where people don't expect them. They may be targeted, like those exchanged by Hells Angels and Rock Machine bikers in Quebec in the 1990s. More often their purpose is to make a civilian populace fear that they or their loved ones could be randomly maimed or killed anywhere, anytime, thus destabilizing a community or whole society by creating mass anxiety.

Pipe bombs are also a favourite weapon of *agents provocateurs*, who pretend to represent one party but whose true purpose is to turn public opinion against that party, and to justify its repression, by committing outrages in its name. Provocateurs don't want to kill a *lot* of people, just enough to scare the rest into co-operating with or voting for a regime that promises an end to the reign of explosive terror.

The FLQ (Front de la Liberation de Quebec) tried the Bolshevik strategy in the 1960s, using bombs to demolish mailboxes bearing the Royal Mail seal, a symbol of British oppression. If they'd stuck to the program it might, like the IRA pub and car-bombs of Belfast, have brought the government to the negotiating table. Pipe bombs are easily concealed and impossible to defend against. Instead the FLQ diversified into kidnapping and murder and gave Prime Minister Pierre Trudeau an excuse to invoke the War Measures Act and send troops to occupy Quebec cities whose citizens were not happy to have Canadian soldiers patrolling their streets, but were relieved not to be blown up simply because they wanted to mail a postcard.

# I.E.D.

Given the amount of dynamite stored in carelessly secured lockers on construction or logging sites, Canada's west coast has been a relatively non-explosive locale, compared to Quebec, where criminals seem to have a *penchant pour le bombe*. Quebec even produced a celebrity bomber, Yves 'the Apache' Trudeau, a rogue freelance biker, rumoured to have rigged a big new TV set with explosives and had it delivered to a motel room where rivals of the gang who contracted his services were hiding. Mom was right; watching TV can be *really* bad for you.

Vancouver's contribution to *An Explosive Geography of Canada*, (eds. Kayman & O'More, Sea-Four Publishing, 2015), is disposed of in a few dismissive pages; an alleged 'gangland' theatre bombing in the 1930s and the unexplained demolition of a stone lion in front of the old courthouse in the 1940s. Our most significant explosions were masterminded in 1982 by the so-called Squamish Five, who blew up a BC Hydro substation on Vancouver Island, (damage: $5 million, no casualties), to protest the proposed Cheekeye-Dunsmuir power line. Then they drove a van full of dynamite to Toronto and detonated it in front of Litton Systems, a company that made guidance telemetry for U.S. cruise missiles. Back in Vancouver, they teamed with radical feminists of the Wimmin's Fire Brigade to firebomb several outlets of Red Hot Video, a chain of VHS retail porn purveyors proliferating in the city. Red Hot got cold feet and folded its lurid tents. Score 1 for the WFB.

The bomb that destroyed Air India Flight 182 over Ireland in 1985 and killed 329 passengers was hidden in a stereo tuner placed on the plane by Sikh extremists at Vancouver International Airport, along with a bomb on another flight that exploded in Japan's Narita airport, killing a baggage handler. Sikh separatists were responding to the Indian government's crackdown on their activities the year before. Score o for Khalsa for murdering 329 innocent people to vent their political spleen.

Vancouver's apolitical criminal class prefers using gunpowder to propel bullets in the direction of business rivals. Local gangs, even bikers, eschew the high explosive mode of self-expression. Maybe they've twigged that the significant characteristic of home-made bombs is their unpredictability. Yet the pipe bomb endures as a feature of the Vancouver scene.

In 2010 an unexploded pipe bomb was found in a West Vancouver school and in February of 2011, a man walking his dog in West Vancouver's Burley Park found another near the playground where teenagers gather to party. On July 11, 2014, New Westminster Police responded to the 100 block of Agnes Street to deal with a pipe bomb spotted at the rear of a building. They called in the RCMP Explosives Unit, who determined it was "a viable explosive device," removed it and blew it up in a "controlled detonation." They deduced it had been there "for an extended period of time" and "it is not believed it was left to target any specific individual or location." A relief to local residents, though the phrase *controlled detonation* makes you wonder if the Explosives Unit is staffed by guys who used to plant cherry bombs in their sisters' doll houses.

Early in November of 2012, just after Halloween, several suspicious objects were found in stations and on tracks of Vancouver's SkyTrain light rail commuter system, mainly on the New Westminster line. The devices were cobbled together—a thing that looked like a pipe bomb, a similar thing with two small empty propane tanks attached. None blew up except when deliberately disintegrated by the bomb squad. No group or person claimed credit or responsibility. Their purpose seems to have been prankish rather than political; to paralyze the system, drive Translink Security batshit crazy with overtime searching the lines and spread general fear for the hell of it. Clean air activists would hardly target Vancouver's mass transit system. They'd blow up car dealerships.

# I...E.D.

October, 1966, one week before Halloween

In Swede Johnson's garage, half a dozen of us are leaning against walls and benches—never against the car—discussing which girls at school might be knocked up and by whom, swapping accounts of epic streetfights and listening to the inevitable motor-mouth who has total recall of every dirty joke he's heard since kindergarten. Swede is at the over-lit workbench, casually spinning the long chromed handle of a bench-vise big enough to pulverize a human skull.

When the steel jaws are backed-off two inches, he places a fourteen-inch length of steel pipe, capped at the bottom, between them and holds it while he carefully reverses the handle in slower circles with his left hand. The upright end of the pipe is scored with threads that gleam dully in the bench light. Below the threads, a wrinkled swatch of black electrician's tape masks what can only be a hole drilled for the fuse.

The yeah-I-fucked-her confessions, the so-I-kicked-him-in-the-nuts bragging and what happened to the traveling salesman whose car broke down so he had to share a bed with the farmer's daughter—are all silenced as if someone snapped the arm off a 45 record player. Swede rests a white plastic funnel, the kind our mothers use for baking, in the open mouth of the pipe. With both hands, he reaches up to the top shelf over the work bench, brings down a coffee can and places it gently on the scarred oil-stained wood.

Cigarettes are squashed hard on the concrete floor. I can feel the hot coal of mine through the thin sole of my cheap boot. Howie lights up, saunters out to the driveway in the autumn mist and leans against Mrs. Johnson's rockery. As his acolyte, I should join him, feign disinterest, but I want to see what happens next at the bench.

A dissociated part of my brain reminds me what Swede and his fellow hot-rod mages do here, what all those unlabelled containers lining the shelves on three sides contain. This garage is a mad scientist's lab of explosive fuels. I am not just watching a bomb being made; I am *inside* a bomb, a complicit ingredient, fuel for its fire. If it explodes here and now, my personal envelope of skin and flesh, the blood-pulse in my ears, my hopes and dreams, my memories and thoughts, everything in me that wants to make love to a woman, write one good poem, and learn to play the guitar, will be blown to proverbial smithereens, literally *dis*-integrated. That's if I'm lucky. If I'm not, after the explosion my crippled bleeding body will be burned alive in the resulting fire.

All of us are so afraid and so determined not to show it that our expelled collective terror coalesces into a separate presence, invisible but palpable. The *smell of fear* was a pulp fiction cliché before I was born, but I know it. It is greasy metal, leather, sour sweat, a fart-whiff of shit, gasoline, and the harsh spice of gunpowder. Despite it, we all lean forward as Swede tips the can and trickles powder, tinged rusty brown in the light, into the funnel. No one breathes, but we all smell the Angel of Death's aftershave in the close air, lingering like the perfume of a girl who broke up with you when you stood her up because the guys were meeting at King's and there might be a battle so you had to be there, or because you might see Swede's pipe bomb before it exploded.

At last Swede sets the can back on the bench. He does not tamp the powder, but wipes the threads with a glistening rag before slowly screwing on the cap. In unison, we exhale and inhale. A guy pulls a smoke from behind his ear and gropes for a match. Swede looks like he is wondering if he has time to brain him with a big Craftsman wrench before the garage becomes a smouldering crater. The guy is one of those who gave me the stink-eye, so I'm not sorry for him when he turns as red as the car, snaps the unlit smoke to the concrete and crushes it like a bug that just crawled out of his cuff.

Howie drives me halfway home because he has a boner for a girl who lives up in Forest Hills and is in some of my classes. I am his Pandarus, an innocuous boy from school who can call on her, albeit accompanied by an older friend who is so obviously a hood that if he called on this fifteen-year-old girl alone her father would have cops on the way before he got past the nasturtiums bordering the lawn. She does not invite us in, where we might have prolonged contact with her parents, who would read us like the Book of Revelations. Sensibly, she entertains us on the front steps. Bored with watching him flirt while she simpers, I cut out and walk home where the garage is not full of explosives.

October 31st, 1966.

Like more than five hundred other North Van youths, while my mother is distracted dispensing candy to costumed children squealing "Trick or treat!" I sneak out and walk down through the traditional Halloween night rain to the Edgemont Village shopping strip. For some years, North Van teenagers have assembled here on Halloween to toss eggs and insults at RCMP officers in yellow egg-resistant rain slickers. It's usually a collegial event involving mild vandalism and mutual raillery. Some officers, it is rumoured, volunteer for the duty for the same reasons teenagers attend; it's a harmless occasion to blow off steam.

In previous years, heavy rain has doused this informal event, driving the small crowd homeward early. This year, the rain is light, so three or four times the usual turn-out of young people fill the streets. Veteran hoods like Howie and Swede lean on their gleaming cars at first, but when they sense they are not, as in Halloweens past, controlling the action and their precious hot-rods might become targets of a large and unpredictable mob, they slink sullenly away into the night, huge V8s growling impotently. This crowd is dominated by fifteen- to seventeen-year-olds and despite my friendships with older grease-balls I am part of it, inexplicably having forsworn Brylcreem for the evening.

I have been living a double life for two years, greasing my hair, ostensibly to hide its length for school and to maintain my low perch in the pecking order of North Van hoods, then letting the shaggy mop loose on the weekends to hang out with people my age, listening to Bob Dylan and the Rolling Stones instead of James Brown or Dion and the Belmonts. This night, I have unconsciously chosen a side.

After customary showers of eggs sold out of shop back doors by venal merchants of the village, the plate glass window of the Totem Five & Dime is imploded by a thrown brick. Fires erupt in dumpsters. More windows crack and shatter under erratic volleys of rocks and bottles. Cops trying to secure the scenes are pelted with garbage. Wading into the crowd, wielding heavy flashlights and nightsticks with grim relish, they toss dozens of us into jail-bound paddy wagons.

I mouth off at a giant Constable in passing and am instantly decked by a casual backhand sweep of his flashlight. I'm dazed but dragged free by friends. One of the guys mounts an overturned garbage can to deliver an anarchist harangue until he is over-run by a wedge of yellow capes and heaved into a police cruiser. We surround the car. A girl that one of my best friends will later marry climbs onto its roof and kicks its flashing lights to pieces before she too is shoved into the caged back seat.

Determined to free our friends, we batter the headlights and windows with rocks and bricks. A defending Constable has his pants yanked down, ripping the shoulder strap of his Sam Browne holster. Radios squeal like blow-torched pigs. From all directions cops converge in a panic because he has *lost control of his firearm*. We flee the furious phalanx like runners dodging bulls at Pamplona, but this is no fiesta. The village looks and smells like a war zone, an apocalyptic landscape of broken glass and burning garbage.

I stumble home with nothing worse than a lump on my head. For weeks, newspapers and magazines run long features, breathlessly analyzing the riot as yet another symptom of the plague of 'troubled youth' breaking out in Western civilization. Some of us are interviewed, asked what we are rebelling against. Shrugging, we give versions of the answer Marlon Brando gives the girl at the soda counter in *The Wild One* when she asks that question, *"What've ya got?"*

The morning after, I realize that amid the crackle of glass and snapping flames, the chanting, screaming, crying and swearing, the head-rush animal roar of inarticulate frustration finding release, I didn't hear Swede Johnson's pipe bomb. Neither did anyone else. All talk at school is of the riot. Nobody gives a damn about one explosion in a park somewhere, however loud.

Pranksters or fanatics, lone bombers are still with us, like the Unabomber who sporadically terrorized the U.S. between 1971 and 1995 with mailed bombs, and suicide bombers cynically recruited from among desperate widows by Islamic radicals. But for most of us who were at the Halloween Riot in 1966, the bomber had become the kind of alienated maniac hiding behind a political cause Joseph Conrad portrayed in *The Secret Agent*; a malevolent sociopath whose power to hurt and terrify innocent people ultimately only feeds his own ego.

That night in 1966 we discovered a power greater than gunpowder. We learned that a group of unarmed politically innocent young people could defy a system of public order our society accepted as monolithic and immutable. Blind as newborn cubs to the long view of history, none of us knew what we would do with that power, but we knew that for us, the days of the lone outlaw were done and a new era of collective activism had begun.

**Acknowledgments:**

Some of these pieces were previously published in somewhat different forms in the following literary magazines and journals, newspapers, and other types of publications: "Village People," *The Vancouver Review*, "A Walk on the Wild Side," *The Vancouver Review* (WCMA award), re-published in Pearson Educational Readers Choice textbook, 2013); "Imaginary Geography," "Bad Haircuts," "The Skin Trade," "Finding My Marbles," "Last Call," and "*!(boom) Pipe Bomb" in *subTerrain*; "Raincity Style," in the *North Shore News*, "Prozac.calm," "Sukiyaki," "Delivering the Apocalypse," "A 29 Hand," and "Crash Test Dummy," in the *Vancouver Sun*; "Roadkill," in the *North Shore Outlook*, "Last Resort," *The Vancouver Review* (WCMA Gold).

**About the Author:**

John Moore has worked as a book reviewer, book columnist, wine reviewer, writer of general features, the occasional dash of news reportage, and various magazine articles. His writing has been featured in the *Vancouver Sun*, *B.C. Business*, the *Vancouver Review*, *subTerrain*, the *North Shore News* and numerous other west coast periodicals and won several West Coast Magazine Awards. He is also the author of a trilogy of noir-ish novels set mostly on Vancouver's north shore: *The Blue Parrot, Three of a Kind,* and *The Flea Market.*